HARD TIMES

For DOnald

from

Larry p Brown Jr

Enjoy the Book

10-16-07
Date

HARD TIMES

✦

A Non-Fiction Memoir

JAMES P. BECKOM SR.

iUniverse, Inc.
New York Lincoln Shanghai

HARD TIMES
A Non-Fiction Memoir

iUniverse books may be ordered through booksellers or by contacting:

iUniverse
2021 Pine Lake Road, Suite 100
Lincoln, NE 68512
www.iuniverse.com
1-800-Authors (1-800-288-4677)

ISBN: 978-0-595-44512-7 (pbk)
ISBN: 978-0-595-68852-4 (cloth)
ISBN: 978-0-595-88839-9 (ebk)

Printed in the United States of America

Contents

Acknowledgements

A Thank You Note to the Meriwether County Sheriff's Department

I would like to thank Sheriff Whitlock and the Sheriff's Department of Meriwether County, Georgia for helping me so much. They now have a new county jail, but the old prison camp where I served my time is still there. They use part of it as office space. A few weeks ago I was able to go through the old prison; the same old bars and cells are still in place. It really looks the same.

I was able to go down and take pictures of Sheriff Whitlock and the prison. I asked him if he would allow me to put both him and his deputy in my book, since they are a part of the prison where I served my time.

Before becoming the Sheriff of Meriwether County, Mr. Whitlock was a fireman. He must be doing something right because he has been the sheriff there for twenty-five years.

I have always tried to stay out of the way of the law, but I must say Sheriff Whitlock is a good man. When you meet him, you feel as though you have known him for a while, or at least that is how he made me feel.

It's amazing that the town of Greenville, Georgia still exists. Most of it is still the same. The old work camp is even there too. On the front cover of my book I have Sheriff Whitlock, a picture of his car and the deputy dogs; they are all there to represent my capture.

I served my time in prison in 1956. I thought the Sheriff's Department, the deputy, Bruce O'Neal, and I getting together, as we have done, would be helpful in bringing my time in prison back into remembrance. I am now 74 years old. When I look back on those days, I realize how much really happened. When the dogs were chasing me, the scent of a bear got to their smell and they went after the bear instead of me. His scent was so much stronger than the scent of my clothes that the dogs lost me. I guess I owe some thanks to that bear for side-tracking the dogs as he did. One thing that I was not counting on happened though—later on, the bear wound up chasing after me! That is not a situation that I would ever want to be caught in again.

As we talked about this, I told the Sheriff I would like to see a movie made about my time in prison. About a year after I was released from prison, Bruce O'Neal came. Bruce knows all about my escape and the dog chase.

Every word I have written here is true and actually happened just the way I tell it to you. Fifty years sure was a long time ago, but I still have my parole papers and I'm sure that somewhere in those old prison files, my records can be found.

Once again, I would like to thank Sheriff Whitlock, Bruce O'Neal and the deputy for helping me bring my prison time back to life. I also want to thank the owner of that beautiful bloodhound photographed with us; he sure did do his job of pinning me down! Now, Bruce O'Neal is the Director of Public Works of Meriwether County. He was a deputy sheriff and came to the work camp after I had gotten out. He knew the dog, Togo, that chased me in the woods. Bruce is the one who knows all about the camp and who helped me get the book started.

My thanks go to Sheriff Whitlock, Bruce and the deputy for supporting me in this endeavor. Thank you very much.

Introduction

My name is James Beckom, Sr. I would like to take the time to thank all of the people who buy and read my book. I thought a long time before I decided to write this book, and I also prayed about it. I have been working for the Lord for the past few years of my life, and it makes me sincerely happy. So, you can be sure that every nickel that comes from this book will be going to good use.

After the publishing of my book, I will be going back to singing in churches and learning to play my guitar and banjo better. With the time I have left on earth, I want to start a ministry and devote my life to working for God.

Although I have been through many troubles and deep waters in my lifetime, I still consider myself to be a good man in spite of it all.

I love the second half of my book. It is called "Spiritual." When you read it, you will see that there is not anything in the book that is not going on in this world today. So, I hope you enjoy the book and tell other people about it.

It seems as though my entire life has been a hard road to travel. Thank God I am free from that old kind of life. I travel the road, now, that I refer to as, "The Gospel Road to Heaven." With my works, my faith and trust in God, I can go as far in Christ as I allow myself. There is no limit to God's glory.

When God blesses you, He expects you to bless others with the blessings He gives you. If God blesses you spiritually, physically and financially, and you do not share your blessings, then you are robbing God of His glory. You should share all of your blessings, no matter in what form it is He blesses you. If He has healed you from sickness, then you should share your blessing. Share your financial blessings with the poor and needy.

Remember, if this book falls into your hands, tell others about it. If this book blesses you in any way at all, share it with others. If they cannot buy one for themselves, let them read yours. That is the way Jesus would have you do. Remember that when Jesus walked this earth, He shared everything He had with all of us. When you share my book, you are sharing in part of God's ministry. Good deeds bring good blessings your way. When you plant fruitful seeds, you get fruitful food to eat.

I know this book will bring plenty of joy your way. There is something in the book for everyone, young and old alike. I must warn you that you may need a Kleenex, as you embark upon reading this book about my journey in life. God bless you, and I pray you are blessed by this book.

1

Life on the Farm

Mother & Father   **Myself**

This is the true story about my life as a child living on the farm. I am going to take you as far back as I can remember.

I grew up in a rather large family that consisted of thirteen children. There were eight boys and five girls. God works in mysterious ways. He had to have known that my father would need all of those hands to help out around the farm.

In the year 1939, at the age of seven (which was the required age to start school), we lived in Raymond, Georgia, a small town outside of Newnan. I remember my first day of school vividly.

Picture me barefoot and skipping down the aisle on the way to my seat, when suddenly I get a splinter in my foot! The teacher put me on her lap and pulled the splinter out, and boy, was I crying! She must have been annoyed by my wailing or either she felt sorry for me (one of the two), because she gave me a jam and butter biscuit to soothe my tears. She sure knew how to get to my heart, because that more than did the trick.

It was after that I earned the title of "teacher's pet," as a result of the jealousy of the other children in my class. All their teasing didn't mean anything to me, as long as I had my jam and butter biscuit. Food was hard to come by back then and that was just what I needed. It did more than soothe my aching foot; it soothed my growling stomach, too.

Not long ago my brother and I went to see if that school house was still there, and it was. So, we took it upon ourselves to take a peek through the windows. We saw that all of the benches, chairs and desks had been pushed into the corner.

I said to my brother, "Perry, look, there is the chair our teacher used."

It looked as though all the chairs and benches were still there, and sixty-six years have gone by. Boy, how time flies!

I remember there was a house up on the top of the hill that my brothers and I would go to in the morning. The woman there would give us each a buttered biscuit, which was something we were greatly excited about, seeing as how food was so scarce.

Back then, some people had nice clothes to wear, but unfortunately, we all did not have that luxury. The majority of the people in our town fell into the category of those that were less fortunate. As you can imagine, my family and I were a part of that majority.

Back then there was very little food or money to be had. If a person had one hundred dollars in those days, they could have considered themselves rich. I remember a couple of my sisters wearing skirts and other clothes that my mom made out of White Lily flour sacks. At that time, I thought those dresses were pretty although the girls who had to wear them didn't think so. I know much better now, and I can understand why they felt the way they did. Hard times today are a lot better than hard times then.

I remember my mom also made quilts back then for all of our beds. I still have one she made, of many colors. My mom was always making something. Many times I wonder how my mom and dad made it through those days, because times were so hard. No matter what came their way, they always made sure we made it through. How, I still don't know; it had to be by the grace of God.

I remember when I was about ten or twelve and times were very hard. I remember having to take Dad's old shoes, which had holes in the center of them, and pack them with paper just so they would fit me. I would also put cardboard in the center, inside of the shoes, to cover the holes. People now have no clue what hard times really were. Times have changed so much, since Mom and Dad's time.

You see, I now have a roof over my head, a nice truck to drive, food on my table, shoes on my feet and clothes on my back. My house may not be extravagant and my truck may not be the one I want. I may not have all the different foods I would like to have, or the shoes I would like to wear, or the clothes I want, but I have come a long way by the grace of God alone.

As a young lad back in school, I can remember other kids laughing at me for wearing my dad's shoes. Little did they know that they were all I had, not to mention the fact that they kept my feet warm. Some of my sisters and brothers did not realize the hard times we went through back then. Today, things seem to be more or less handed down to you on a silver platter.

I can remember once, at school, I tore the seat of my pants. Mom had to patch them up with a "White Lily" flour sack patch. When you tell others of those hard times, they may look at you as though you were crazy.

I'm leaving out a lot of my life story, and that is mainly because I cannot remember everything. However, there is a lot in this book that will give you some idea of how hard times were.

I used to sit and think that if everybody else had hard times like we did what a sad world it must be. It seems things always have a way of getting better. I do thank God that our children do not have to go through the hard times we had to go through.

I remember we had little food and very little money back then. My dad, along with my brother Bobby and I, had to catch a ride to Macon, Georgia to help my Uncle Ted and his boys pick up Irish potatoes. This was how we got money to buy food for my mom and the rest of the household. Dad always left Milt and Perry at home with mom and the others because they were the oldest boys.

We started out walking, hoping to catch a ride to Macon. We spent the night in an old house that was about to fall down. We would get so cold and hungry in that house at night. No one would pick us up as we walked.

Finally, an old 1931 truck of some kind gave us a ride. There were apples on the back of it. We were only allowed to eat one each, but we ate until our bellies were full and, boy, did we get a belly ache from that. The worst part about it was that we did not even know how to count, and we just kept on eating. All we could think about were the others at home and how they did not have much to eat.

We finally got to Uncle Ted's house. We helped out in the field, pulling potatoes out of the ground. Uncle Ted sent some food and money back home to Mom and the others so they would not starve, because we had to stay for a week or two. It felt good to have a place to sleep and food to eat.

We helped Uncle Ted and the boys finish up with the pulling of the potatoes. They were doing pretty good with their crops. They had a lot of stuff to gather up from their fields. Uncle Ted had a big farm. He even had people from the chain gang out there working.

Finally when we got back home, we had to gather up our potatoes. We would bury our sweet potatoes in pillows with dirt so they would not freeze. We would have them all through the winter. At least we would not starve.

Dad found a job for the winter in Newnan, which was about twelve miles away. I can remember how he would put some kind of bags around his feet and shoes and walk to Newnan to go to work. He made only twelve dollars a week. Talk about hard times! Now you must know why I call my book "Hard Times."

By the grace of God, we did make it through the winter. We were so glad to see spring arrive. We started farming our crops again. It was harvest time once again! I remember how we would load the wagon up with watermelons and other produce and take it to Newnan where we would peddle the things we had. We would sell it all, but by the end of the day, our Daddy would have spent all the profit on moonshine, and we would go back home with nothing. Dad would be drunk and asleep in the back of the wagon.

We would get home late and our mother would always ask, "Did you get the flour, lard, meal and other things I asked for?" We would have to look at Mama and tell her that Dad spent all the money we made on moonshine. So, we had to have cornbread and syrup for breakfast. It was like that for a long time. Then, as the family grew, we would move to different farms.

I remember something that happened at one of the farms we were working when I was about twelve years old. Dad used to call my mother "Bunk." When we were working in the field, he would say, "Bunk, it's time to go start lunch." I can still see Mama going down that long hot road. She would be carrying one baby in her arm and leading another one by the hand. The old mule would let you know when it was time to eat lunch. She would start snorting, and it was always around 12:00 noon when we put the animals away.

Of course, I was hungry too! Mama would yell, "Ya'll come on now while it's hot." She did not have to ask us twice, either! She would always cook black eyed peas or butter beans and have buttermilk for us to drink.

After we ate, we would rest a little and then go back to the fields. We would work until the sun was almost going down. Then dad would say, "Bunk, it's almost time to start supper." So, Mama would start down that long hot road again, carrying one baby and leading the other by the hand. In a little while we would all go to the barn and feed the animals.

Mama would call out the back door, "John, come on, supper is ready." A lot of times we would have cornbread and buttermilk for supper because it would fill you up. We had a long table. Mama would sit at one end and daddy at the other. All of the kids would sit on either side of the bench. It started out with just eight of us, and then there were thirteen.

We lived about six miles from the store. Daddy would send my two older brothers, Milt and Perry, to the store to get kerosene for the lanterns. When they got down to the mail box, I would holler at them, "Can I go with you?" They would tell me to come on, but I was not thinking straight.

When I got back, Dad was waiting for me with a limb off the oak tree. When he got through with me, I could not sit down without a pillow!

On the same farm, my brother Bobby and I, who was just two years younger than me, would go in the cane patch, topping cane and fighting. We heard a noise one day, through the bushes, and looked up and saw Dad with a big oak tree limb again. Boy, I did not know if I could stand that pain again, but he gave both of us a good whipping anyway. As far as I was concerned, that was enough, so I tried to walk the line from then on.

Later on that day, Dad gave each of us a nickel except me—he gave me a half dollar! So, we all went to the store in a mule and wagon. Each of us would get an ice cream. My brothers and sisters would gobble theirs down and then turn to me asking, "Ain't you gonna eat yours?"

I would say, "Yep, but I want to look at mine for a while." That was in case it would be another year before I got one. Then it would begin to melt, so I would just eat it.

They wanted to know where I got that half dollar. I would tell them, "If you had helped Dad run off that whiskey last night, you would have one, too."

There were other people standing there who heard me, so Dad said I was just joking and told me to give him the money. The other people just laughed it off.

Dad had bought a young mule and hooked him to the plow with Biggon. Biggon was a big black mule with a white spot on her forward; she was the best mule we had. That little mule would pull that big double plow almost by itself. Old Biggon would just tag along and rest while the little mule did all the pulling.

I had an uncle named Tiny. We called him "the chicken man." He had a hole in the left side of his head as the result of someone hitting him with a hammer because he was stealing chickens.

One Saturday Uncle Tiny asked Dad to let him ride the young mule, and Dad told him that he had better not, because the mule was not broken. Uncle Tiny insisted that he could ride anything, and he jumped on the mule. The mule threw him on top of the barn. He said, "How am I going to get down from here?" Daddy told him to jump. From then on, he never rode that mule again.

Uncle Tiny was a lot of wind. One night, we heard a noise out in the chicken pen. My daddy got his shot gun, went to the back steps, and let out a yell. Out came Uncle Tiny and started running through the pastures. Dad started shooting the gun in the air and asked who was out there. Uncle Tiny started yelling, "Don't shoot, don't shoot." He later denied that it was him, but from then on, he was careful about whose chickens he stole.

We had lived at this place for a while and Dad began to drink a lot more, mainly because he was making his own liquor. I remember one night, Dad was drunk and he had gotten bad about jumping on Mom. He had the shot gun pointed at Mom's stomach. Milt and Perry had gone to get Uncle Wilbur, another one of my Dad's brothers. Uncle Wilbur would not come any further than the mailbox. So, the sheriff came and took Dad to jail.

When he got out, he was better, but only for a short while. Soon, he started making moonshine again. I sat with him one night and held the jug, letting it run off a little at a time. It took two hours to run off a gallon because it was a small still.

Then one night, Dad was drunk again, and started after Mom. Every time he got drunk, he would do that. Milt was the oldest, and would always try to stop Dad. Milt ran out to the back porch and Dad hit him with a gallon of liquor. It knocked him down the steps.

Milt went to dad's brother, Uncle Grady, and Milt never tried to help Mom after that, when dad was attacking her.

The next morning, Dad sent me over to Uncle Grady's to get Milt. Uncle Grady was the only brother of Dad's that was not afraid of him. He brought Milt and me home and told Milt to start working. Uncle Grady had a talk with Dad, and Dad told him that he would straighten up, but that did not last long either.

When we lived there, we were farming on halves with the government. We had a tornado while we were living there that killed some of the milk cows and other animals. The government pulled out of the agreement and took our hogs and mule. They left Dad two mules.

Old Red was the one I started plowing after that happened. One day, late in the evening, I decided I was going to ride Old Red home. So, I jumped up on Old Red and he took off running. Let me tell you, when I got off that mule, I was so sore I could barely walk. I never tried to ride that mule again.

After the government pulled out of the agreement, we had to leave that farm. We moved to a place called Banning, Georgia. There was a cotton mill there at the edge of the river. They had a spring and it had the coldest water you could ever drink. I put on a lot of weight, and everyone teased me about it. It had to be that spring water that made me fat, but soon I lost the weight.

I remember it was there that I took my first bite of chewing tobacco. After doing that, I sat down in the swing. It wasn't long before I was drunk. The next thing you know I was lying on the ground, and boy was I sick!

Later, we moved to Griffin, Georgia. We lived a long way out in the country. We farmed on halves with a man named Harry. He rode a big red horse out to the farm. He would have an overcoat on in the winter. He rode that horse about ten miles from town. I remember one Saturday, Mama and I were walking to town. I was carrying chickens and she was carrying eggs. We would trade them for flour and large black-eyed peas.

I remember getting off the school bus. You could just see our house way down the road. We got there as quick as we could and always ate black-eyed peas and bread. Next, we would head to the fields to work.

Then we moved into town. Some of my brothers and sisters went to work in the cotton mill. After that, things began to get better. We ate things that were totally new to us.

I remember some of my cousins would gather on the front porch and play the guitar. Robert, Leroy and Melvin would all sing as they played.

There was a creek that ran down beside the road and it was full of rats. They used to pour hot water in the holes and the rats would come out into the creek. There were bloodhound dogs that would always chase the big rats and hold their heads under water until they drowned.

Later we moved to Manchester, Georgia. We moved into a cotton mill village called Callaway Cotton Mill. I guess I was about fourteen, then. Some of my brothers were working, so again, we ate better and life was better. But we had not gotten away from hard times just yet.

I still remember one time, there was a long hill down below us. One day I was riding a bicycle down that hill and the chain came off, and there I went. There was nothing but a dead end waiting for me, so I ran into a briar patch to keep from running into the creek. I did not know which one was going to be the worst, but I chose the briar patch. Boy, was I full of briars!

Dad wound up quitting at the cotton mill and they made us move as a result.

We moved about ten miles from town. We moved into a big house up on a hill. Dad started farming a little. By then, there were three of us working in the cotton mill: me, my sister and my brother, Perry. I quit school at age fifteen so I could work in the cotton mill.

Things were getting better. We ate better and had better clothes to wear. Dad was like a bloodhound, or at least he had a nose like one. He was plowing in the field and at the end of the field, there was a patch of woods. I worked on the night shift but I had gotten up. I was looking out across the field and I thought Dad had been out there for a long time. So, I walked out to where he was. I found him there with a bottle of moonshine and drunk as a skunk.

The worst thing about my Daddy getting drunk was that he would always take it out on Mama. I know my Daddy loved Mama, but I guess it was easy to take it out on her. When Dad got drunk, there was just something that took over him. His Dad had treated our grandma the same way. Dad's other brothers didn't hit on their wives. I guess Daddy just picked up that habit from Granddaddy. Of course, the others' wives would all fight back. Mama was never the type to fight back.

I loved my Dad, but he was hard to deal with when he was drinking. While we were living there, my oldest brother, Johnny, got in trouble with the law. He was on lookout, watching for two of his cousins. Someone called the law and they picked my brother up, standing on the corner of a street. They said he had just stolen a car. He didn't have a car, but they found the car later, and blamed it on him. By the time he got home from jail, there were thirteen kids and I was working in the cotton mill.

I remember we would go the movies on Saturday and we would stay until night. They would have to run us out of the movie theater. We would have to walk about eight miles to get back home. There was an old church and a graveyard on that dark road. People would say it was haunted. It was always so dark on that road that we could barely see each other. Every time we got to that church, we would ease on by and then take off running.

There were other times we would have to walk home late at night. The manager at the theater knew us, so he would let us stay late every Saturday night. We would always watch western movies just about all day long, and then at night, there would be different movies on—movies about Big Foot, Wolf Man and bears. One night, Bobby, Tommy and I were watching Wolf Man and, of course, after the movie was over, we would have to walk that long eight mile road home in the dark.

When we left the theater, we walked so close together that night. When we got to the church, we took off running as usual until we got to the creek to take a break. We were sitting at the creek resting, and instead of hearing a bobcat, this time it sounded like limbs were breaking. It was almost like something was walking towards us coming out of the woods. We were already scared after watching the Wolf Man movie at the theater. We got real quiet; then I said, "What did that sound like to ya'll?"

We were all thinking the same thing—that it might be a black panther, bear or even Big Foot. I said, "Well, we ain't gonna wait around to find out." So, we cranked up our feet and took off running out of there. We were running so fast that there was no way anyone or anything could catch up with us. But even that night didn't stop us from going to the movies on Saturdays.

I was fifteen, Bobby was thirteen and Tommy was eleven. Bobby and Tommy still went to the movies but I had to start working at the cotton mill. When we could, though, all three of us would go to the movies and I would treat them to popcorn and drinks. Things happened that way for quite a while. Daddy, Bobby and I still had some farming to do together for a little while, and we would go just about everywhere with Daddy.

I remember on several occasions, Dad and his friends would meet down at the creek. They would set out their fishing poles and bait their hooks with bread. They were fishing for catfish and any other kind of fish that would latch on to the hook. My dad would always take me and Bobby along with him to the creek. After they got through setting their poles out, they would roast a pig and a chicken over the fire. Bobby and I would watch it, and they would play poker all night long and drink moonshine. Some of them would get so drunk that they'd get angry and start fighting. The rest of them would always break up the fights.

On those nights we didn't get much sleep, because most of the night we were up looking out for snakes. The next morning, all those who did get to sleep would wake up, drink some coffee, eat, and then check their poles to see if they had caught any fish. They always split the fish they caught equally among the others. Then, they would start playing poker again. As they played, Bobby and I would be fishing. Later on that evening, the game would break up and everyone would go home, all except Bobby, Daddy and me, along with a few other guys.

One of the guys named Bob had his shirt off, and he called himself a "bad dude." He was just looking for a fight. There was a guy walking down the same road we were on, and he overheard what was said. So, he came over and started talking.

Bob walked up to the guy and said, "Hey, is your name Bill? You look like a pretty good man. I'd like to let off a little steam, so how about you and me fight a little?"

Bill said to him, "Hey, man, you're drunk, so that wouldn't be a fair fight."

Bob said, "Don't worry about me, man." Bob was known to be the meanest man in town.

Bill told him, "Well if you insist on fighting somebody, Bob, it had just as well be me, but I don't want to hurt you. So let's just make it a friendly fight and no one gets hurt, no matter who wins."

But Bill was unaware of the kind of guy Bob was. Like I said, Bob was a bad one and he never lost. Bob liked to get out there and slug it out with his fists, and if he didn't win one way, he would win another. They went at it, slugging it out.

Bill knocked Bob down four or five times, but Bob didn't stay down. Bob was about drunk and he had been playing poker all night long. Bill was fresh and ready to go.

Bob finally realized he couldn't win this one. Now, this is what I meant when I said Bob wouldn't lose. Bill said, "Bob, let's quit; you can't whip me like you are. If you want, we can try again when you're sober."

But Bob wouldn't hear it. He got up after being knocked down about ten times. Like I said, Bob was a bad dude. When he finally got up, he went and got his rifle and said, "The fight ain't over until one of us is dead."

Bill saw that Bob wanted blood, so Bill took off running. My dad tried to stop Bob but he said, "Nobody whips me like that and lives to tell about it."

He told dad to get out of his way. I tried to talk to him also, but he looked wild. Bob told me and Bobby to help him find Bill and he would pay us. He told me he was going to kill Bill and put his body in the river.

We started looking for Bill. I was looking beside the river and in the water. I saw bushes moving and looked over in the creek, and there he was. He was scared to death. He begged me not to tell Bob where he was, and I said I wouldn't.

Bob hollered and said, "Have you seen him anywhere?" I told him that Bill was gone and he nowhere to be found. Bob finally agreed to go home, thinking that Bill was gone.

I asked Bob if he would have really shot Bill if we had found him, and he said, "Like a rabbit."

Bob was just so mean and everyone knew it. Bob climbed up a tree one time, forty-five feet in the air, and people would bet on whether he would jump or not. This man didn't know what fear was. He wasn't scared of anything or anyone. He would dive from that tree and land in a big hole of water. Everyone called him "diving board" for doing that. The hole was only thirty feet deep. When he hit the water, he would come right back up. Now, was he brave or not? So much for the strong and the brave!

The reason Daddy liked for me and Bobby to go places with him was because we were kind of like him. We were rough necks. One time, in the field at the end of the road out by the woods, Dad found some moonshine. Bobby and I went out there because Dad had been there for a long time.

We took a shot of moonshine, and it was strong.

Dad and Bobby were always hollering at each other, and always trying to see who was the strongest. That was only when they were drinking. Bobby was always trying to outdo Daddy.

Bobby would say, "James, come on and help me."

I would tell him that he was doing all right. Bobby had bit off more than he could handle; Dad was strong in his arms.

We had a boxing ring set up behind the house, and we would always try to whip everyone who came up there to box. I guess Bobby and Tommy were the best. I had a hard punch but I still wasn't that good at boxing.

We had a watermelon patch behind the cow pasture. One evening, I went down there and picked a watermelon and took it to the branch. I put it in the water and lay down and slept while it cooled. When I woke up, it was cold, and I would bust it open. I got the heart of it out and ate it. I was so full, and it was so good and sweet. I would then head back to the house and at 8:15 P. M. I would go to work in the cotton mill.

I met a girl named Joan and I thought she was so beautiful. Every time I was on a break, I would go talk to her, and when she looked at me, my face would turn red. I would forget what I was going to say to her. She was nineteen and I was fifteen, but that didn't matter to me. She was always friendly, and being friends was all she had in mind, but not me. I was in love with her, or what some would call puppy love, but I thought it was the real thing.

A guy named Adam came to work there that had just gotten out of the Army and right away, they started talking. The next thing you knew, they were married. She stopped talking to me so much after that. Their marriage didn't last long because he left her, and he stopped working there.

She had his baby, and she was devastated by what happened. That made me so mad at him. I talked to her dad, and he told me that he had told her that Adam wasn't the right one when she started seeing him. He had a fast line to shoot her, and she was taken in by it. I was too young for her, but I did ask her to wait for me. This finishes the story of my life on the farm. Talk about hard times—my family and I sure had some!

2

My First Love, At Age Sixteen

As time went on, I met another girl at work. Her name was Joyce. I guess I was just too young for Joan and Joyce. I wish I had been at least eighteen, but my age didn't' stop me from talking to the girls.

I worked in the card room and Joyce worked in the drawing room. I would push six cans of drawings up to Joyce and she would take that big round cane and put it underneath a machine that would suck it out and put it into a ball. From there, it would move up the line.

When I carried the drawings to her they were like a string of cotton, only it was in a whirl. That was when I got sweet on Joyce. She was a lot friendlier than Joan. I later told her that I like her and she told me she liked me too. What she didn't know was that it made my day to hear her say that.

It got to the point that I couldn't keep my hands off of her, even at work. I was putting my arms around her and things like that. She would just turn around and smile at me when I did those things. I don't think she really thought anything of it, but I sure did. She was a very pretty girl and she knew it, too. She seemed flattered to have a young boy falling for her.

Since I was only sixteen, I didn't have a car and I wanted to ask her out on a date. One night when I caught up with her, I started flirting with her. Every time I tried to ask her on a date, I would freeze up and couldn't get the words out. After several attempts she turned to me and said that she would love to go out on a date with me. When she said that, I almost passed out because I thought she would turn me down because of my age. She thought I looked older than sixteen.

For our first date, we went to the movies. She asked if I had a car and I told her I didn't, but that I was old enough to drive. So, she said she would just meet me at the movies in Manchester, Georgia on Saturday night at 8:00 p.m. I told her that was fine with me. I kissed her on the cheek and she told me I had better get back to work.

When we got off of work, I would walk her out of the building and she would let me kiss her on the cheek. I would be in blue heaven the rest of the week. We started sitting together on our lunch break and we would talk and eat together.

I didn't really know what was going on in her mind, and honestly I didn't really care, because I was in love with an older girl who liked me too. Boy, I couldn't wait until Saturday night came. We worked on the third shift. When we got off from work on Saturday morning, I told her goodbye, kissed her on the cheek and told her that I would see her that night. You can imagine how my day was. I couldn't sleep; I was up and down all day. I just couldn't wait until that night.

Finally the day passed, and I got dressed and started that ten mile walk to Manchester. I finally got to the movie theater and had to wait a little while on her. I saw her drive up across the street and she walked across the street toward me. I just stood there watching her with my mouth open. I thought to myself, "Oh, my God, she looks like a movie star." She was so beautiful. She had on jeans and a blouse, and short high heels. Her long black hair was moving as she walked.

You know how you felt when your dad threatened to whip you. That was how I felt when she walked up. My legs were so weak I could barely stand on them. I had double dated with a couple of girls from the church, but I never had dated anyone like Joyce.

She came up to me and I said hello, and took her hand and kissed her on the cheek. I told her she looked beautiful. I thought, "If only my dad, mom, brothers, and sisters could see me now with someone as pretty as Joyce."

We got our tickets, got some popcorn and drinks, and went inside to the theater. I think we both felt the same thing right then. We agreed to sit in the back row where the lovers sat.

The movie we watched starred Humphrey Bogart, but I can't really remember the title. I looked at her and she smiled at me. We looked on each side of us and saw that no one was really watching the screen because they were busy making out (what we called "necking" back then). We looked at each other again and smiled.

I told Joyce that I had never kissed a girl before, besides on the cheek, of course. So I didn't really know how to kiss, but she sure did. It went on from there. We couldn't have even told you what the movie was about. When she got through kissing me, my head was spinning.

Joyce knew something was wrong so she asked, "James, what's wrong with you?"

I told her I must have eaten too much popcorn and she laughed at me and said, "You'll be all right."

We left the move and went to the PYE joint. It was a place down by the railroad station. My oldest brother had married a girl who worked there—her name was Janie.

We ate a hamburger and played the jukebox for a little while. Some of the guys in there kept looking at Joyce, and she looked at me and said, "Let's go, James."

I think she knew that if one of them came over and started flirting with her, I would have to say something and then a fight would have to take place. I knew I was a young boy, or at least younger than most of the guys that were in there.

Joyce took me home and we sat outside in her car for a while. We started necking a little. Joyce didn't hold back from a kiss but I could still tell something was bothering her. She helped me to grow up a little bit and I will always remember her for that. You know, you never forget the first kiss you had.

After that, Joyce and I became very close to one another. I was beginning to fall in love with her, and I think she was getting feelings for me too. Wherever we went when we were together, people would always ask if we were married. We were only dating, of course, because I was much too young to get married.

I finally got my first car. It was a 1939 Plymouth, and I sure did love that car. Now, when we went out, we would always take one car and leave the other one at the cotton mill. Joyce and I were getting in pretty deep and I could already tell that one of us was going to get hurt—I just didn't know which one.

One night we were kissing each other and then she started crying. I asked her what was wrong. I was getting older at this time and was starting to really care about her and the feeling was mutual. We both knew we were falling in love with each other.

I had always heard about love and younger boys falling in love with older girls, but now I was experiencing it for myself. I didn't want our love to end. We had been together for over a year and a half, and it wasn't long before I would have to go in the Army.

I didn't want to have to go and leave her. I wanted so badly to take her with me, because I was afraid that I would never find anyone else like her again in my life. But would she go with me?

I decided I would have to ask her and see, because I could never go off and leave her. I loved her so much. Now, I know this was my first love, but to me it was more than that. It was kind of like the first car that you get. But when you love a human, it is so much more than an infatuation. I don't know why I was so worried about it, because we had a few months left before I had to go in the Army.

That night we went to the drive-in movie. We barely watched the movie because we were so busy kissing and holding on to each other. We acted as though it was our last time together. I felt like something was wrong. We had been together since I was sixteen and now I was just a little over seventeen. I felt like I was a grown man. I grew up faster than a lot of young men.

You know what is so funny about this love story (I guess you would call it a love story because I really did love her) is that no one knew about it. Not even my folks—my mom, dad, brothers, or sisters—or anyone knew about it. Joyce and I tried to keep it from everyone because of our age difference.

You know how you feel when your dad is about to give you a spanking. Well, that is the way I felt right then. I felt so alone, like I was about to lose her. If I did, I didn't know what that would do to me. I didn't blame her for the way things were between us. There may not have been anything wrong at that time, but I couldn't shake the feeling.

That night at the drive-in, she told me she wanted us to be alone that night. When she said that, I knew something had to be wrong. That night, neither one of us could sleep. So instead, we just held each other tight all night, because we knew it was going to be the last night we spent together.

When God made man and woman, He knew what He was doing. He knew that young people were going to fall in love and get their hearts broken. That is why He made it so that we could come to Him when things like that happen.

Joyce and I both knew that we were wrong for the way we were living. We didn't care, because we were both young and so in love. We didn't know what was going to happen next, so we just lay there all night. At least I didn't know; Joyce knew exactly what was going to happen. She just didn't tell me until later.

It has been fifty-five years since Joyce and I were together. I must say, I didn't really think about Joyce for a long time before I started writing this book. As I write it, I go back to that last night with her, and tears will just start falling. I did not know how much I really loved her until I started writing.

I have had other girl friends in my life since Joyce, but Joyce was my first love. I will never forget our first date, and our first kiss, and how that kiss made my head spin.

My problem with love is that when I fall, I fall hard. To just think about losing her hurts badly. It is so hard to say goodbye to someone that you love.

Now that I am older and looking back on it, it hurts even more. I never thought I would be telling the world about my love life, but here I am. I wouldn't take anything for the memories I hold in my heart of Joyce and me. The last night that Joyce and I spent together will always be mine to cherish, and it hurts when I think of our departure. She told me she did not mean to let it go as far as it did.

"What do you mean?" I asked her.

I told her that we had waded through deep water together and could not stop now because I had come to love her and loved being with her.

She said, "Don't stop loving me now. I love you too, but you are so young. When you and I started talking and became friends, I did not see any harm in us seeing each other, but I did not mean to hurt you. I must tell you something, James."

I started to say something but she put her hand over my mouth and asked me to please listen to her.

She told me she had a boyfriend coming home from the war, and once he got back, they were to get married. She told me that she did not think things would turn out the way they did when we first started talking, and that we had to break it off that night. She said that if her boyfriend found out we had been dating, he would hurt both of us because he was very jealous.

She said, "James, you are young and will be going to the Army before long. You will meet other girls and fall in love all over again."

I told her I would never forget her and that I understood, but that I would always love her. She was so sweet. I told her I didn't know how I could make it without seeing her and she said I could still talk to her at work. If you have ever been in a situation like that, it is hard to let go, but I went along with her. I hoped that everyone in the cotton mill would keep their mouths shut.

One night, my boss came over and introduced me to Chuck, Joyce's boyfriend. He told me that the job I was doing used to be his, and that he would want it back. Chuck asked me to swap jobs with him, and he said that he and Joyce were getting married.

I shook hands with him and told him he had a fine girl, and that Joyce had talked about him a lot. Joyce was sitting on pins and needles by this time. Chuck and I worked side by side and became good friends. I still got to be around Joyce a lot; we would kid and laugh together.

One night Chuck, Joyce and I double dated together. The girls went to the bathroom together and he told me he wanted to talk. He said he knew about me and Joyce. He told me to listen. He told me he knew I was young and was going into the Army, and maybe I would go where he went. He said that there was the possibility that I could get killed. He said that he did not need to know what happened between Joyce and me, that he understood and probably would have done the same thing. He said, "Forget about it, but don't ever go near her again. Do you understand?"

I needed to say "yes" or "no", and I looked at him for a while. He said, "Well?"

And I said "Okay."

I told him that if I had known she had a boyfriend, we would have just been friends, and that I was sorry. He told me to forget about it and that he wasn't mad—but to remember what he said.

It wasn't long after that before I had to leave to go to the Army. When the time came to leave, I told everyone goodbye. As I stood there, Joyce and I stared at each other. Chuck came over and said, "Well, since James and Joyce have been good friends, let's give them some privacy."

After they left, we said goodbye and told each other we would never forget each other. We cried a little.

Chuck came back in and wished me luck. I didn't see Joyce again until I got out of the Army and went back to the cotton mill. By then, my family lived in LaGrange.

Since I had worked in the cotton mill, I thought I would check to see if there was an opening I could fill. When I walked inside, I couldn't believe who I saw first. It was Joyce. She hadn't changed a bit. There was another guy sitting there also.

The Joyce I know got up and came and hugged my neck. We both said hello at the same time. By that time, her husband came out of the bathroom. He just stood there and looked at me.

He told me he thought he had gotten rid of me when I went to the Army. I told him hello, and he told me he did not have anything to say to me. Joyce told him to be nice. Chuck told her he could not be nice, because I tried to steal her away from him.

I told him he obviously had not forgotten about that. He told me if I knew what was good for me, I would leave, because the mill was about to close. I asked them why they were still there.

Chuck got mad and threatened to beat me up. I told him it shouldn't take a big guy like him to need company to beat up a little guy like me. He asked me what I did in the Army, and I told him I was in the special MP forces. He and his buddies finally sat back down.

Special MP's were the police they would call in when the job was too rough for the regular police. They all sat there and looked. I told Joyce goodbye and that she was still as pretty as ever. She got up and hugged me, and then I left.

As I went out, I looked back and stuck my thumb up at Chuck and his friends and told them to take it easy. I thought to myself that I sure did bluff them. I had to, or they would have beaten me up. I didn't see Joyce anymore.

Some years later I went back to Manchester and tried to find that town. I guess they had done away with it because it was not there. It was a small town, but I won't give up looking. My brother said he thought he knew how to find it. So, we are going to go down there and spend the day pretty soon.

I do not expect to find Joyce, though, but you never know. All I can do is ask around. Joyce and Chuck may still be living there, or maybe someone can tell us what happened to them. I am really just looking for her just to see her to say hello.

3

Time in the Army: April 1, 1950

Myself in the Army

When I was seventeen and a half, I knew it was Army time. Back then, they drafted you at age eighteen. So, I decided to go in early, and because of that, I got to pick the part of the Army I wanted. I chose the Signal Corps. I started my training at Camp Gordon, Georgia. After training, I got a three-day furlough.

When I got home, my oldest brother Milt had gotten married. I walked in the house and he said, "Janie, come here. I want you to meet my little brother." She stuck her head around the corner; she was so shy.

I was the first one of my family to go in the Army. Mom and dad had quit having kids by then. In total, there were thirteen kids—eight boys and five girls. My mom still had a house full of kids, though, and I guess dad was still finding his bottles of moonshine at the end of the field.

When it came time for me to report back to the Army, I said goodbye to everyone and left. I was on my way to the war in Korea. This all happened around 1950.

I reported back to Fort Jackson, South Carolina. On the day before we were to leave for Korea, I heard my name called over the loud speaker. They wanted me to report to the CO, and I did. He told me that he needed two men to go to Germany. I thought about it for a minute, and realized that if I went to Korea, I might not ever come back, at least not alive. Something inside told me to go to Germany, so I told the CO I would go.

I was shipped out to a camp near New Jersey as I waited for the ship to come in headed for Germany. We spent quite some time there, and I got the chance to visit New York for the first time. I saw Broadway and everything, but I saw that New York wasn't really any different than Atlanta. The streets were full of people, and a lot of them were bad looking people. They didn't even know what grits were!

Every morning we had to get up and clean our areas, and then the rest of the day was our time. We had a lot of time on our hands.

Our ship finally came, and it was a cargo ship. There were 5,000 women and kids on the ship, and 2,500 troops. When you are talking about a lot of water, nothing could compare to the ocean. The last thing you saw leaving New York was the

Statue of Liberty with her hand up in the air. Then it was gone and we were on our way to Germany. It took sixteen days and nights.

We had a curfew that allowed us to stay on the deck until dark. One time I was standing on the back of the ship and it would go way up in the air and then come back down causing the water to hit you in the face. It was the same way on the front of the ship. The ocean was rough and people were getting sick everywhere. You would be sitting at the table and your food would start sliding to the other end of the table. When you looked out of the side windows, when the ship rolled over on its side, you could see fish through the glass. I was glad when we got to Germany.

When we arrived, we had to wait until trucks came to take us to the train. We went to a guest house and we all got drunk on that strong German beer. We got into a fight with a bunch of Germans. One guy with us was a boxer. He was knocking them through the window. The war might have been over, but we got in on the tail end of it.

Some of those Germans did not like for us to talk to their girls. So, here came the military police. They loaded us up in a truck and carried us back to the train station. Now, we all had a bad headache. That was our first fight.

We got loaded on the train and headed to Kelley Barracks in Stuttgart, Germany. That was the third largest city in Germany. The train traveled beside the river all the way. They called it Red River, and it was beautiful. When we finally pulled up to a huge building, it looked like a world by itself. We loaded up on a bus and headed up a long mountain to Kelley Barracks. When we got there, I signed up for an education program. I was training for combat during the day and going to school at night. Since I only went through the fifth grade in school, I figured I needed it.

I decided to go downtown, and you could see where it was bombed. That Air Force knew what they were doing when they bombed. People were living in holes, tunnels and burned-out buildings.

I went into a jewelry store and met the dream of my life. She was a fifteen-year old blonde named Monica. Her parents and I hit it off right away. I was in love before I knew it. I thought she was an angel. You know how it is with young love—I was only seventeen and a half, and across the ocean from home in Germany. I was going to school at night to finish out my education. But I quit school so I could spend more time with Monica.

When I got off guard duty every day, I went to Stuttgart where Monica was. It got so bad that I was slipping out under the fence at night to go see her. I had a guy pick me up down from the MP. gate. Finally I got caught, and they sent us all out on a field trip. By the time we got back, she was gone. I could not find her anywhere. So, a buddy and I started running around downtown in the underground tunnels.

There were bars there that had not been damaged by the bombing. They don't call them bars in Germany, they call them guesthouses. When I was over there, you could see how the city had been destroyed by the bombing, but it has since been rebuilt. Everyone says it is a beautiful city again. It was still in ruins when I left there in 1952 to come back to the States.

Back In Training—In Snow Country

One time we were out on a field trip up in the mountains. You could see a city below. Snow was waist deep in some places. In order to take a bath, we would line up in a long line and when we got up to the hole of water, we would take our clothes off and jump in the pool. It was about 10 degrees below 0. We did that every morning, and then we would go get in the chow line.

They had me standing guard at an ammunition dump. One night, it was as dark as pitch, and I heard a noise. It kept making a sound like a coughing noise, and in a few minutes, it was right near me. It was a bulldog. Boy, was I glad to see him! Here is an eighteen year old, over in a foreign country where a war had been fought. You talk about being scared! Well, I was! I kept that bulldog with me all night and I didn't walk around. We sat down next to a tree. That way, I could see or hear anyone who came up.

I still had not forgotten Monica. I was planning on going back to Stuttgart soon, because my time in the Army was just about finished.

I had met a girl in Harrisburg, Pennsylvania, when I was stationed up in Camp Kiama, New Jersey. Her name was Connie, and she was very pretty. We went together while I was waiting to go overseas. They lived in White Lake, Texas. Her dad was in the oil business. Her mother had to bring her to Pennsylvania for her health. We were planning on getting married when I came back home. But when I met Monica, I quit writing to Connie, because my mind was elsewhere. I knew that it was not right, but what can I say? That is the way young love is.

Connie was waiting for me when I got back to New York, but I did not go to see her. I called her and told her that I was too young to get married because I had a lot of living to do before I settled down. So, I let her slip through my fingers. I say that now because I may have had a good life with her father in the oil business. But that was another time and another place.

I got out of the Army and went back home, but things weren't going good for me at all, so I went back in the Army. I thought they were going to send me back to Germany but they said that they couldn't do it then. They sent me down to Camp Polk, Louisiana. So here I was—stuck in the swamps.

We went out on a field trip for three months and when we got back, I knew I didn't want to stay in the Army. When we got a leave and it was time to go back, I didn't go back. I went to San Diego, California, where one of my brothers was stationed in the Navy.

As I was standing in front of a bar in San Diego, a drunk came out and asked me to light his cigarette. As I was giving him a light, a police car pulled up. They put him in the car, turned and looked at me and said, "Where are you from?"

I said, "Georgia."

They asked me if I had any money and I said, "No sir, I just got into town."

They said, "Come on, you are under arrest for vagrancy." So I spent the night in jail. It was so packed in there that there was no place to sit down. I finally found a place to sit down, and then there were people crawling around me on the floor. One guy looked at me and came crawling over to me. When he got close to me, I kicked at him. They said he was kind of a "funny" guy. I said, "Just keep him away from me."

The next day my brother, Tommy, came down and got me out.

Life in the Army

Tommy and I went down to Tijuana, Mexico. Tommy was dating a girl from there. Tommy was tall, had a good physique, and a wide grin. Tommy wasn't someone you would want to fool with, unless you wanted to get beat up. He would walk down the street with a tee shirt on, looking as if he owned the street.

There were Mexicans everywhere. Some of them would reach out and touch his arm and say, "Big Man," and then laugh. Tommy would turn around, look at them, and laugh. Tommy had big muscles. He was a good looking fellow. Of course, he knew it.

He had a big left hook that would lay you out. He was a very proud man and it took God to bring him to his knees. Thank God he got saved about three months before he died.

Now, I also had a mean right hook. All I needed was just one punch and you would be out.

Tommy and I went into a bar. I liked Mexico and their music and, of course, their senoritas. A girl came over while we were in this bar to take our order. Tommy knew enough Spanish to order for us.

Every time someone special would come in the bar, a dancer would come over to your table and dance for you. We were

Americans, so we were considered special. They think that all Americans have money.

Their dancers wore blouses and skirts with tap shoes. They held little round balls in their hands. As they danced, they would tap their feet and pat those balls in their hands (castanets), get close to you, and go around and around you. All the time, they would be looking at you. As the dance came to an end, they would sit in your lap with both arms around your neck and pop those balls.

By this time, Tommy and I had had enough to drink to make us sound bad. We were having such a good time that we didn't want to let the girls go, and they didn't want to leave. I would have loved to take one of them home with me. Tommy and I loved the music and the way the girls danced.

We kept holding them in our laps, cuddling up with them. It was the girls' jobs to entertain us, but they seemed to be overdoing it. So, a crowd of Mexican guys started coming over to our table. Since the Mexicans were coming over to our table, the girls left.

The guys were all around us. I told Tommy I thought it was time for us to go. Tommy told me to pick up my beer bottle and get up slowly. By then, the Mexicans were just too close to us. We couldn't explain anything to them because neither of us could speak Spanish.

We did try to bluff our way out, but we couldn't handle all of them. By now, we were backing out of the door. A group of about 20 Mexicans, including some outside, had gathered. They were talking to each other. Whatever they were saying must have worked, because they all backed away.

We laughed it off and patted them on their shoulders. They nodded their heads and kindly waved at us. They had seen Tommy in the bar before. When we left, we went to see his girl-friend. He had not seen her in a week, so she was really upset. When she finally calmed down, we left.

Tommy took me to the shipyard and showed me the big air-craft carrier ship. It looked like a city. Tommy told me that his job was to flag the planes and jets in as they approached the landing. He said that sometimes he had to flag and wave them off.

After we ate, Tommy left to go back to the base. We said our goodbyes and I started on my way back to Georgia.

This will be hard for you to believe, but I started walking all the way from San Diego to Georgia, and finally caught a ride in the desert. There was a rest stop about 50 miles out of San Diego, from where I got another ride with some strange looking people. I was thankful for the ride, but one girl in the car would keep putting her hand on my left knee. She then got in the back seat and ran her fingers through my hair. I was really glad to get out of that car.

They were going on down the road, and I could have gone with them. But I needed to get to Georgia, so I got out.

When I returned to Georgia, I went to work in the cotton mill. It wasn't long after that before the GBI man was there at the mill to pick me up for going AWOL. He took me in hand-cuffs back to Fort Benning to be put in the stockade.

While I was in the stockade, I met a man they called "Rat." A rat in the stockade is someone that tells the guards, captain, and warden what goes on inside the building. He told me that they were going to give someone a "blanket job." I did not want to participate in that, but I was told that if I didn't help, I'd get it too.

After the lights went out, we all gathered around him. Some of the guys had shoes and ball bats, and others used their fists. My part was to pull the blanket real tight. One guy put his hand over the mouth of the guy in the blanket so he wouldn't make a noise and be heard. I felt so bad for that guy. The lights came back on and we all ran back to our bunks.

The MP checked each one of our hearts. When they checked mine, one said, "Here is one." Boy, my heart was pounding hard.

They took me and put me in the hole (solitary) on bread and water only. When my time was up to get out of the hole, we started to work under the shotgun.

One day, one of the other guys and I talked to the guard with the shotgun and asked him to put it down because we didn't want to hurt him. He was such a young guy, so he put down the shotgun. When he did that, we took off.

It wasn't too far to the railroad trestle. We climbed up on the railroad trestle and man, was it high! I looked down at the river and almost fell off. When I got up on top of the railroad track, I was so weak I could barely walk. It took a little while to get my legs to move again.

We slept out in the woods that night. We had pine straw to use to keep us warm, but we still got cold. The next morning, we were in Phenix City, Alabama. We were wet and cold by then, and hungry.

There was a hospital across the road from us. We had to wait in the woods all day, until dark. About 10:00 P. M. that night, a car drove up in front of the hospital.

A man and a woman got out and left the keys in the ignition. We ran over to the car, took it, and drove to Nashville, Tennessee. We ran out of gas, and neither of us had any money. We were dumb to ever think we could get away.

We found a little money in the car and got something to eat. We left the car and caught a ride all the way to Nashville. We were still a long way from where the other guy with me lived. We started walking in and out of the woods until we reached where he lived.

The MPs and the GBI were out front. We went in the back door. They didn't seem to be watching the back door. I think if I was looking for someone, I'd be watching the back door as well as the front. We knew we would get caught sooner or later. His mother hid him and told me I'd have to leave, so I left. She did give me something to eat, but no money.

I didn't know where I was going but I started out walking. I would go in and out of the bushes behind houses. I had no intention of getting caught (at least, I thought). I kept on walking and finally ended up in downtown Nashville somewhere. When it got dark, I found a car that was open. I got in it and started looking for some money. I heard someone coming, so I lay down on the seat.

Both doors opened and two men jumped back and looked at me. One said, "Well, what do we have here?"

I said, "Sir, I'm sorry for meddling through your car. You see, I'm a long way from home, and I'm broke, cold, and hungry. I was looking for some money so I could get back home."

I didn't tell them that I was AWOL from the Army. I saw no reason why I should. I told them I didn't want any trouble—just wanted to go home. To my amazement, they were both preachers.

One of them said, "Do we call the police or what?"

The other one said, "Where are you going?"

I told them I was going to Georgia.

They talked it over and the first one said, "You seem like a pretty good fellow, so we'll take you out to the main road and then you can catch a ride home."

They took me to the main road. Then these two men of God prayed for me and gave me some money. One gave me his overcoat and wished me luck, and then they were gone.

I was in the mountains in Tennessee and didn't really know which way to go. I guess it didn't really matter, because either way I went, I would run into the GBI or MP. So I decided to head back to Georgia, since that is where I was from.

Finally, I made it to Atlanta. I walked about 10 miles to where my brother lived and spent the night there. I later went to downtown Atlanta and was standing at a bus station and two plain clothes GBI men walked up.

One of them said, "Are you James Beckom?"

I turned and looked and said, "Well, well, what do we have here? You guys must be GBI men."

They pulled out their badges and said, "You are AWOL from the Army stockade and you are worth $50 to us."

So, of course, I put out my hands and got cuffed, and off we went to Fort McPherson in Atlanta. The camp was ten miles out of Atlanta in the East Point area.

I got there at 12:00 midnight with it raining very hard. They gave me a shovel and told me to dig a 6x6 hole 8 feet deep. I started digging.

When I finished, they said, "All right, fill it back up." So I put the dirt back in the hole.

By that time, it was 5:00 a.m. I got cleaned up and they gave me a uniform to wear. The cap was so big it kept falling down in my eyes.

The MP took me on the train back to Ft. Benning, Georgia, back under the shotgun and work detail. In a few days, the captain called me to his office and said, "Beckom, I don't think you're going to make it back in uniform, so I'm going to give you an undesirable discharge."

I was told that after six months, I could take another test and go back in the Army if I would like to do that. So, I didn't have to go out on work detail, but we still had to get out of bed at 4:00 a.m. every day.

After we'd get dressed, we'd have to go outside and do P.T. (physical training). We had a little sergeant who would make us do the "chicken hop." Boy, that was hard to do! You would have to put your hands behind your neck, squat down and do the duck walk. Most of us fell on our faces.

It wasn't long before I was given my discharge. There were two sergeants who got discharged at the same time I did. The Army strips you of all your rank, and you leave the same way you came in.

They loaded us on a truck and took us down to Columbus, Georgia and then they put us out on Main Street. They made sure there was a crowd of people watching and then handed us our discharge papers. The MP just stood there smiling at us, not saying a word.

The people were just watching us. It didn't bother me. I just looked like everyone else who was walking down the street. So, I found a bar and a mug of beer and gave myself a toast to the Army.

I said, "Good riddance, good luck and goodbye to the Army—and thanks a lot! I am free at last."

4

Time in Prison and My Escape

(Sentencing Day: July 13, 1956)
(Paroled: May 22, 1961)

Meriwether County Prison

Myself In Prison

After I got back to LaGrange, Georgia, I started running with a wild crowd. I was restless and I didn't know what to do.

During all this time, my brothers and sisters were growing up fast. So, I decided to go and take the test to go back in the Army, but while I was taking the test, I changed my mind. I didn't know, at the time, that I was about to have six years of my life taken away from me. I was about to make the biggest mistake of my life.

I began to drink a lot, and things began to get out of control at that point. One night I was in a club out on Highway 27 in LaGrange with some friends, drinking moonshine. My brother, Dick, had told me not to go to the club that night, but I went anyway.

After it got late and everyone was drunk, I had trouble with some of the people in the club. My head was spinning and pounding. After that, I must have passed out and the next thing I remember, I woke up and the police were pulling me through the window. Apparently, I had gone to sleep by the jukebox, and tried to open the window to get out. Then, I fell back down on the floor.

The police had a twister on my left hand and wrist. They pushed me over the hood of the car and had a pistol pointed at my head. The police in LaGrange were very tough. I didn't know why they were mad at me because I was only sleeping and had not done anything wrong. They chose to make an example out of me.

They put my picture in the newspaper showing the cop holding the pistol to the back of my head. My mama kept the picture for a long time.

I hated getting in this kind of trouble because my brothers and sisters were still in school. I know that when something like this happens, it is hard on the family.

They kept me in the county jail for ninety days before the trial. The sheriff and the GBI told me they had about nine counts they wanted to clear off their books. I didn't have an attorney, and there was no one to advise me of my rights. Today they furnish you with an attorney, but they didn't do this in 1956.

They had me for one break-in at the Club. I didn't break in, but since they found me inside, they believed I had broken in.

You would have thought that I would have learned something about life, being in the Army, but this was new to me, and

I was just a country boy. The sheriff told me that if I would admit to all the unresolved crimes, they would let me go with one charge. Boy, was I dumb!

When we got in front of the judge, he asked the sheriff what was the charge against me. The sheriff told him I had just come home from the Army, and it looked like I was trying to hit every store in town. He told the judge they had me on nine counts of burglary.

The judge looked at me and said, "Young man, don't you know better than to do something like that? You are old enough to know better."

I looked at him and said, "Your Honor, they only have me for one count. They told me to sign that paper so they could clear up the old counts."

The judge asked the sheriff if what I said was true and the sheriff told him I was guilty of every count I signed for. From that point on, the judge wouldn't listen to me. He said he had to take the sheriff's word, because he would never lie.

The judge said, "James Beckom, I am going to sentence you to three years in prison on each count, and each count is to run consecutive. You are hereby sentenced to nine to twenty-seven years. You can serve some or all of it. You will be eligible for parole in three years if you don't mess that up and you're good."

My knees buckled under me. I turned and looked at my brother and his head was bowed down. Then they took me away. The law only works for you if you are rich and know a lot of people in the right places. So here I was, about to serve someone else's time. I know my family was hurt, but not as bad as I was. I'm sure the people who put me in prison on false charges got their dues in time. They are all dead now, and whatever God did with them is all right with me.

They put chains around my legs and linked them to my wrists, put me in a truck with two others, and down to south Georgia we went. It took us all day to get there. When we pulled into the Hawkinsville prison branch, I saw dog boys and two guards beating a man. The dog boys are called trustees.

They had the guy's hand cuffed behind his back. The guards were trying to hold him while the dog boys hit him, but he was kicking them and butting them with his head. I found out later that he was the meanest prisoner they had, and his name was Sabao.

Usually the bad ones didn't have anything to do with you, but I made friends with some of the bad guys there. When Sabao got out of the hole, we became friends.

They had a chapel at the prison, and every Sunday we could go to church. The warden recommended that you go. He said it would help us handle our time in prison better. I went every Sunday, and got Sabao to go with me. Most of the boys in there didn't want any part of him, but they had begun to talk about him and look at him. When he caught them looking, they would turn their heads.

One day in July, we were in the field unloading cement off a flat train car. It was hot and those cement bags were so heavy. Saboa asked me if I thought God would get mad at him if he backslid for about fifteen minutes, because there was one guy who was giving him a lot of trouble. I told him I didn't think God would mind if he messed around a little.

He asked the boss if he could fight that guy, and they gave him the okay. They liked to see the boys fight. Saboa said he wouldn't hurt the guy much, just give him a good whipping to shut him up, so they went at it. After that, things got quiet.

One day, we were working at the country club, cutting grass and cleaning up. A big guy we called Mule found a rattle snake and picked it up by the neck, and the snake bit him. Mule started getting weak after that. He thought he could get better without help but he only got worse. The guard finally came and carried him to the camp. The next day he was better.

We were pulling up stumps one day, and Mule came over and told us all to move out of the way. He got in the hole and pulled on that stump until he pulled it out of the ground.

The warden called me to the office one day and told me I was being transferred to the Greenville, Georgia work camp. This was about twenty miles from LaGrange, Georgia. My family didn't live too far from there.

The warden at the camp knew my mom and one of her sisters. My mom's sister told her she would take her to see me at the camp in Greenville, and that is why I was transferred there.

They put me to work under the shotgun. We worked in fields, picking pears and busting rocks. They were all backbreaking jobs. They would give us a 12-pound hammer and by night time, that hammer had better be worn down.

It even got worse in the winter. The guard carried a shotgun and if you wanted to straighten up or get out, you had to let them know. If you got out and then stopped shaking the bush, the guard would let loose with buck shots. So we had to remember to always shake the bush. I was serving my time, but I didn't like it one bit. I was railroaded into being in prison and there was nothing I could do about it. So, I tried to settle down and do my time.

The walking boss at the camp knew my family but didn't show me any favors. Slowly, though, he started to soften toward me.

One day, we were putting up a fence and he told me to hit a stake he was holding with the hammer. I was scared I would hit his hand, but I did it. The hammer fell off the stake and hit his hand. He reached for his gun and I told him that I was sorry, and didn't mean it. He looked at me and told me to do it again, but to be careful. So I tried again and got it right that time.

From that point on, he made me the water boy. One day the warden told me to step out and after everyone else was gone, he told me he was going to put me on truck detail, so I did that for a while.

One morning, he called me out again, and told me to go with Tommy, who ran the front-end loader that loaded the truck with rocks. He told me to stay with Tommy and learn how to work the front-end loader since Tommy would be getting out soon. I learned how to work it and became really good at it. After that, I loaded everything and carried it to its destination.

One day, we went to Warm Springs, Georgia and headed up a high mountain. The old Ford truck almost didn't make it. It was down in low gear, and if it wasn't for the truck behind me pushing me, I would have rolled all the way back down.

When winter came, things got bad. Winter didn't have mercy on anyone. I made it through the first winter, and then spring came. There was a new guy by the name of Jeff who started talking to me. I guess he singled me out.

5

Time in Prison—Part 2—My Escape

Myself, The Bear, and Capture

Jeff started talking to me about breaking out of prison. Here I was, with about three years left to go before my parole came up, and I let this guy talk me into running.

When the time came to run, he chickened out. I felt as though I had gotten a raw deal anyway, so I took off and left without him. I slept in the woods my first night, but later I went out to the edge of the woods.

There was a house across the field, and I saw a woman hanging out clothes and little children playing in the yard. I guess they must have seen me too, because it wasn't long before I heard the dogs barking. So here we go—me running and the dogs on my trail.

I found a creek and got down in the middle of it so I could lose the dogs, and I did. That didn't last very long though. The dogs picked up my scent somehow, and they were on my trail once again. When I watched the movie "Cool Hand Luke," I thought to myself that it should have been my movie, because I actually lived that part. The only difference was that I didn't get shot.

Somewhere down around Woodbury, Georgia, I lost the dogs again, and that night I slept in a cave up on a high hill. The next morning I heard a noise and got up and looked down in the valley. I could see the warden, the sheriff, the state patrol and the dog boy with his dogs. They didn't know where I was, so I started running again. Somewhere on the other side of Woodbury, the dogs picked up my trail again.

No one had ever outsmarted those dogs and their keen sense of smell. One of the dogs was named Togo and the other was Old Sam. They could pick up your scent in the air. The only way to lose them was to find a creek or some kind of water and get in the middle of it. They could not track you if you had not touched anything.

I needed to find some clothes so I could change, so I went back out to the edge of the woods. I found an old house where a woman had hung out some clothes on a line. I sneaked up to the house and took some of the clothes. I knew that as soon as that family missed those clothes, they would know they were taken by an escaped convict, and boy was I right!

Later on that evening I heard Togo and Old Sam barking. I knew they must have picked up my scent, so that motivated me to move faster.

I stayed in that cave on top of the hill again that night. For some reason, it seemed to be warmer inside the cave. Later on, I realized that there must have been something else living in that cave; however, it must have been out looking for food, for I had not seen it.

There is no telling what could have been calling that cave home. Pine Mountain Valley was an animal world, so to speak. There were plenty of black bears living around there. Black bears don't usually bother you unless they are hungry or you bother them. But there was no time for me to worry about a bear. I had to get some sleep.

I had to break into a café to get some food, and I knew they would find out about that and be on my trail again the next day. I figured all the hairs that were in the cave would throw the dogs off for a little while, giving me more time to run.

So there I was—deeper into the woods. I was sitting down to rest and I heard something above me, and I looked up to see what it was. All I could see was something that was black, and it was moving around. I thought it had to be a black bull, cow or even a black bear. I got up and started walking, and as soon as I did, I heard those dogs barking like crazy again. So once again, I started running.

I had to get more clothes because the dogs had gotten the scent of the ones I was wearing. I was thinking maybe the dogs would pick up the scent of whatever animal was living in the cave and they would lose me. I also knew that if I was able to get far enough out of the way, I could lose them all together. Losing those dogs was the only chance I had of making my escape a success.

I thought it would be great to get to Atlanta, because there were many places I could hide in the city. But there was no way I could get out on the highway right then, so I figured I should probably wait until things died down. In the back of my head, though, I knew those dogs would not give up until they found me. I knew it was time for me to get out of those woods, because I needed to find some new clothes.

I started looking for a house with a clothes line outside and while I was searching, I heard a noise. I saw a house, and there were people outside loading up their car. I guess they were getting ready to take a trip. I sat there and waited until they left, and made sure I didn't hear those dogs on my tail, and then I went out to the house.

I peeked in the windows to be sure no one else was in the house. When I decided the coast was clear, I broke a side window and went inside the house. I didn't want to break into these people's house, but at the time, I had no choice. My goal was to get exactly what I needed and to get out of there.

I grabbed a pair of pants, a shirt, some socks and shoes. Next, I went to the kitchen, got some food, and took off. After that, I rested a while.

I must have gone to sleep, because I found myself waking up to the sound of dogs barking, and I knew they had to be Old Sam and Togo. My next plan was to lose the dogs and find a car or truck to steal, and get out of the way. I realized that I had left my old clothes in the house I broke into, and figured out how they were picking up my scent so quickly.

I thought to myself that I had better get smarter. Everything I had done before that was stupid and with every move I made, I didn't seem to get any smarter.

To begin with, running was the worst thing I could have done. I knew there was something in those woods with me, and to have to go deeper into the woods made me nervous. I felt I was being double chased—by the dogs and whatever was living in those woods. But deeper into the woods I went. I also knew that the further I went into the woods, the less chance I had of getting out, because in the long run, a bear would overtake me. I also knew when those dogs got after that bear, that he would go deeper into the woods. The farther the bear went the less chance I had to escape him. I had rather for the dogs to catch me than that bear.

I had no idea where I was. Sometimes, when I heard the dogs, it was the bear that they were chasing and not me.

Now, I don't care how good a dog is, when they run across a bear's scent, it is so strong that they just take off after it. That gave me a break to rest a little while, so that night I slept in the woods. I found a hollow tree and slept in it that night.

I took straw and leaves and put them all around me. I didn't sleep much because I kept hearing a hard breathing sound. I just knew that a bear was around there somewhere. Because those leaves and straw were all over me, he couldn't smell my scent. I told God that my life was in His hands.

The next morning, when I awoke, I looked around and I didn't see anything. When the sun came up, I headed back toward Woodbury. When I got up on a high hill, I saw something big moving up above me, so I went another way.

I had gotten lost by this time and didn't know where I was. While trying to figure it out, I heard the dogs and knew they were hot on my trail because they sounded so close. I knew I had outsmarted them once and thought I could do it again. I was getting tired of running, and it seemed as though I was going in circles. I started to wish I had stayed back at camp. I may not have liked it there, but at least I had food to eat and a place to lay my head, not to mention the fact that I wouldn't have those dogs and whatever it was chasing me.

I figured the animal on my trail had to be a bear or a pack of wild dogs, or maybe even a big foot. It was beginning to get dark and I didn't hear anything chasing me. So, I went down to the water to get a drink because I was quite thirsty. I built a fire and then lay down in the woods. The only light I had that night was the light coming from the fire. I ate what food I had, and then I went to sleep. I used straw and leaves to help me keep warm, along with the fire.

The next morning, when I woke up, I washed my face in the water. I looked around to try to figure out where I was, and then I started walking again. I found a creek a few miles from Woodbury. I knew this was the only way to lose the dogs. I went down into the creek and walked for about a mile or two and I couldn't hear the dogs. I knew I could not be far from Woodbury and that the dogs would not give up on me. I also knew that eventually there would be no more creeks and I didn't know what I would do then to lose the dogs.

I knew it would not be hard for them to pick up my scent the next day when I left the creek. I was hoping to get a ride to Atlanta to go see my brother. That night I went out to Highway

85 in Woodbury and saw a café. I went in the back window so I could get something to eat. I found a bag and filled it with as much food as I could. After that, I got out of there because I knew I need to hurry in order to escape.

I found another branch of water that night and started another fire. I ate as much as I could, and then put my fire out because I heard a noise in the woods. Suddenly, the noise got louder and closer. It was so dark I could barely see my hands in front of me. I had no idea what to expect and didn't know in which direction to run in case I needed to run.

I started walking anyway and pushing my way through the bushes. As the noise got closer, I started walking faster. Whatever was on my trail seemed as though it was breathing right down my neck. It turned out to be a black bear. He must have been hungry because he was chasing me.

Not only was the bear chasing me, but so was Old Sam and Togo. Don't get me wrong—it was a scary thing to have that bear chasing me, but at the same time it was a good thing. You see, a bear's scent is far stronger than that of a human. Because of this, the dogs were thrown off and they lost my scent. They began chasing the bear instead of me. However, at that time I wasn't thinking about anything like that. I just wanted to get out of those woods before that bear caught me.

The closer it got to me, the faster I ran. I ran through briar patches, into barbwire fences, got caught in there, and almost didn't get out. When I was in that barbwire fence, I could feel that bear chewing at me. I could feel his teeth as his mouth would come down beside my head. I just knew that my life was over, but I kept fighting and kicking and screaming, and finally

I broke free. I guessed the bear got caught in that barbwire fence, because I didn't hear him behind me.

I ran until I got up to the highway and saw a car. I stuck out my hand to flag them down so they would see I needed a ride.

They were going really slow, and I knew they had to be the State boys, but I didn't care. I had had enough of the woods. Sure enough, it was the State boys and they pulled over and got out.

"Are you that Beckom boy?" one of them asked. "We've been looking for you!"

All I could say was, "Yes, sir."

"My God, boy, what happened to you? It looks like a bob cat has gotten a-hold of you."

I told them about me running into a barbwire fence, and how that bear was all over me, and how he had been chasing me all through the woods, and how glad I was to see them there, for they just might have saved my life!

They picked me up and took me to the warden at the prison. The warden put me in the hole for fourteen days on bread and water.

After I got out of there, the store man gave me some food to eat. I ate until I was about ready to bust, but it took some time before I got my strength back.

Whenever a prisoner escapes, all the others want to know details. They asked me questions like, "how far did I get?" and, "how did I get caught?" So they gathered around me and got really quiet so they could hear my story.

I told them about everything that had happened to me in detail. I told them how hard it was to lose the hound dogs and how, just when I thought I had lost them, they found my scent again. They sat there so quiet listening to me, you would have thought we were having Sunday school lessons. I told them all about the black bear chasing me and how the dogs chased the bear. I told them about the cave and hollow tree I slept in, and how the bear caught me. I thought that after telling them my story, maybe none of them would try to escape. I guess my escape was enough for a while.

After getting out of solitary confinement, the warden told me that he knew the new guy (he was referring to Jeff) had talked me into running, and that he knew I was really a good guy at heart. He told me that he would let me stay in Greenville because of my mother, but if I got into any more trouble, he would send me away, regardless of his knowing my mother. He said he would send me to a place called Reidsville.

No one wanted to go there because of the reputation of that prison. I told the warden I would not try to escape again. So, I settled down to do my time and I went back to work under the shotgun.

The boss didn't trust me for a long time, and as a result, the next few years were hard for me. It was back to busting rocks in the quarry, using that old twelve-pound hammer. By night that hammer had better be worn down.

When you were busting rocks, the chips would fly all over you, and if were not careful they would hit you. One day, we were down in Chipley, Georgia. We were resting under a tree around lunch time, right next to a railroad. The train came rolling by and it was going really slow. I sat up on my elbows and started looking at it.

The boss saw me and yelled, "All right, Uncle Pecker, I know it's going your way, but today ain't your day."

The shotgun man had already raised his gun and was ready to shoot. The boss told us to go back to work. We had to let the boss know every move we were making, whether we were sitting down or standing up.

Those were hard times, but we made it. Eventually they let me run the front-end loader, and I worked it until my time was up.

They turned me down the first time I came up for parole. One year later, I was up for parole again, and this time they had a new person on the board. It was a woman named Vicki, a very nice looking lady.

When I went before the board, they asked me so many questions, and I answered the best I knew how. I don't think Vicki ever took her eyes off of me. The other three on the board turned me down, but Vicki didn't. She said she could look at me and see that I was not a bad guy.

I told them that I was railroaded into being sent to prison. Vicki felt as though I had served enough time, and she overruled the other three members on the board. She stamped my papers, wished me luck, and sent me on my way.

She didn't know it, but I could have kissed her right there in front of everyone. In a few days I was free to go. There would be no more busting rocks and picking pears. That had been backbreaking work, especially picking those pears.

I was so relieved to be out of there. As I was reliving my escape, I know now that it wasn't a big foot chasing me because I don't believe in that anymore. I think it must have been a big bear, by the way it was breathing. You know how bears breathe hard when they are running. I found out later that there are black bears in Pine Mountain Valley, so I know it couldn't have been any other animal.

A few years before, my grandpa had killed a black panther up there in Pine Mountain. From what I had heard, it was about six feet long. However, I think what was chasing me was a bear. It smelled my scent and the food I was eating. When something is chasing you, especially in the woods, you don't stay around to find out what it is. All you think about is getting out of there.

There I was—an escaped convict running from the law. When people hear of such people on the loose, they get alarmed. They lock their doors and grab their pistols. I wouldn't hurt a fly, but people didn't know that, because some convicts will get violent.

While I was running from the dogs, I was only going in circles. Once I got to Woodbury, it meant I wasn't going anywhere for sure.

I'll tell you, when a man gets hemmed up, he gets like a wild animal. I think this part of my life story would make a good movie. This is one part of my life I will never forget for as long as I live.

I said goodbye to the chain gang and headed home.

6

Life after Prison

I was twenty-six years old when I went to prison and thirty-one years old when I got out. My brother picked me up from prison when I was released. My brother was a preacher, and he had a church in Manchester, Georgia.

I got a job at the saw mill and worked there for a while. I went to my brother's church, joined the choir, and it was there I met a girl. We dated for a while, but you could see she had one thing on her mind—getting married. I had been in prison for five years, had just been released, and I had a lot of catching up to do. Getting married was far from my mind. Because of that, we broke up.

My brother gave up his church in Manchester and got one in LaGrange, Georgia. By this time I had left the saw mill and gotten a job at the RC Cola Bottling Company. Later, I moved to LaGrange and got a job in the cotton mill. I lived with my mom and dad and started going to my brother's church again. I became the lead singer in the choir, but I was not yet ready to get fully involved with the church. I felt as though I had a lot of living left to do.

Some of my sisters and brothers were still at home. There was a girl who was a friend of my sister. I don't remember her name, but she was something special. I will never forget her. I think I must have fallen in love with just about every girl I met.

I finally left LaGrange and I went to Atlanta where my brother, Johnny, lived, so I stayed with him. I went there to find a job. Hard times were still with me.

Every day, my brother would give me a dollar so I could go search for a job. I know now that I would have been better off staying in LaGrange. There, I had a job and friends, not to mention all those pretty girls.

Being up in Atlanta, I was afraid I would get in trouble with the law again. I was running with a rough group again. I thought about how I got railroaded by the police before, and all that I went through when I was in prison. I didn't want to go back to prison, but I stayed in Atlanta.

There was a friend of mine who I met in prison who had gotten out before I did. He offered me a job and an opportunity to learn auto body repair and painting. Now, I had a chance to learn a new trade and possibly make something of myself.

I worked there for a while, until a man called me from Chrysler-Plymouth and offered me a job. They started me off at $200 a week. So now I was on my way, learning a new trade and getting good at my work. I finally became supervisor over other people.

I saved up enough money to buy a 1955 Oldsmobile Holiday. It was a two-door, blue and white, with a hard top. I still had not settled down and married. However, later on I did get married, and we had a son.

I used to go down and see my mom and I would take her down to Pine Mountain Valley to see her dad. He lived in Chipley, Georgia.

When my mom and I got down to my grandpa's house, he told me to come to the back yard because there was something he wanted me to see. So, I followed him back there and he had a hog.

He got on that hog and rode him around in the yard. That was the biggest hog I had ever seen in my life.

There was something else my grandpa wanted to show me in the back yard, so he waved me over. I followed him behind the house, and he had a watermelon patch out there. There were big melons all over. He had a melon covered up with grass, and when he uncovered it, I had never seen a melon bigger than that one. It was as big as a wash tub.

There was no way that one man could pick it up by himself. I told grandpa that I would like to bust it open and eat it. He told me that he was saving it for a special occasion.

We went back to the house and grandpa asked my mom to play a song on the piano for us. She could play the piano really well, and she played a beautiful song. My grandpa was a Baptist preacher, and he found out that I had been going to a Church of God. He told me he knew that I was going to a Holiness church, and that he wanted me to go to a Baptist church because they preached the word of God there.

I didn't have much to say about that, so I just agreed with him, and I told him that I would.

Grandpa loved cigars. I would watch him light them up and he looked like he really enjoyed them. He had a church around where he lived.

I really loved going to see Grandpa—he seemed to have a lot of wisdom about everything. When it was time to go home, it was always hard to leave him.

My grandpa died at the age of 92. He is one man that I will miss dearly, and I certainly will never forget.

One day, when we went to see him, he was on top of the roof putting up shingles. When he saw us, he came down.

He was 88 years old then. Today, at age 73, there is no way I could do anything like that.

My grandpa had been fairly prosperous, and he made sure that Mama finished high school. Mama was a smart woman. She could spell and read anything for you. God rest her soul in heaven.

Later on, I moved to East Point, Georgia. This is where my first love started in Atlanta. I met a girl while my brother and I were living there in a house together. So here comes another love story.

Buckle up, hang on, and let's take a long love trip that I think you will enjoy.

7

A Girl Named Brenda

I met this girl named Brenda when I was running around with my brother in Atlanta. She had a way about her that you could not resist.

One night, my brother Tommy and I were at a place called Bob's Hideaway on Stewart Avenue in Hapeville, Georgia. My brother was about six feet tall, with blonde hair and broad shoulders. He had a big wide grin and was a very nice looking man, especially to the ladies. He could look through a girl without batting an eye. I was just an available guy.

We sat down at a table and a good looking girl came over to our table. Tommy already had his eyes on a blonde cross the room. She was giving him the eye, too. Brenda came to our table and asked if she could help us.

We both looked her over real well. I said hello and introduced Tommy and myself. I told her to bring us a beer and to walk slow, so I could see her walk. She just turned around and laughed. I had no idea that I would be taking her home that night.

I knew right away she had her eyes on Tommy but I did not let that bother me. Tommy and I didn't usually go out together, but this was a nice place. I had been there a couple of times before, but I usually hung out at Dutch Kitchen.

Brenda brought us our beer and hung around with us. She leaned up against me, and then Tommy started talking to her. She kept flirting with Tommy even though, by then, she was almost sitting in my lap. She did not know it, but she was about to drive me crazy. By this time, my arm was around her waist. She didn't even try to pull away—just leaned in more.

Brenda and Tommy were talking the entire time. It seems as though she was eager to get one of us. Tommy knew he could get any girl, almost any one. If he wanted Brenda, he could have had her. She saw that she wasn't going to get Tommy, so she set her mind on me.

Tommy finally danced with the blonde and left with her. Brenda got off work and let me take her home. She sat close to me in the car, like we had been together for a long time. I knew then that she was for me. So, that was the beginning of our love life. From then on, none of the other girls mattered to me.

She stopped flirting with the other men and we dated a long time. I have always felt like she regretted not getting Tommy, but once we started seeing each other, she never mentioned him again. She seemed to be happy with me. Tommy was not one for a long-term relationship, and he knew that Brenda was not a one-night stand.

Brenda and I settled down into a dating relationship. She was exciting and pretty, and a lot of fun. She showed me how it felt for a man to be with someone who really loved him. It seemed that the more we were together, the more in love we were. It seemed that we were on a honeymoon every day. I realized, by then, why no one man could hold on to her.

We went everywhere together. She would always sit close to me and was always kissing on my neck. She loved to pick at me and pretend she was mad at me, just so we could make up.

We liked to go to the drive-in to eat. We would order a hamburger and coffee for me and Coke for her. She'd keep her arm around my neck all the time. She would take a bite of the hamburger and give me a bite. We always ate like that. We never did eat much. She always said we could live off love forever.

I asked her if she wanted to go do other things—like shoot pool or go fishing. She would say no, and that all she wanted was to be loved. I guess that is why I loved her so much. Wouldn't it be nice if we could stay young like that forever?

Three of my brothers and I rented a house together—Tommy, Jack and Larry. Jack and Larry were very young. That is when Brenda met all of my brothers. She would be standing by me but flirting with them. That was her way of being friends.

Larry was in love with a girl down the street. Brenda was always happy and would talk with everyone. There was never a dull moment with her around. She would take me to work and then come at lunch time, and we would have lunch together. Then, she would go to her mother's house until time to pick me up from work. Then, we were off together again. We were like honeymooners.

Brenda said, "We are not ever going to get old."

I had never met anyone like her. She would come in the kitchen, stand in the doorway with her finger in her mouth, flirting with me. The following was the best part of my life with Brenda. So buckle up, and let's go for a ride.

One time, Brenda and I went to North Carolina to see one of her friends. I had a 1959 Chevrolet Impala, and that was a good car. She wanted to go see a truck driver who she said was her cousin. What I did not know was that he was crazy about her.

She told me she was going to tell him that we were just friends. I didn't like that, but I went along with it for a while. Every time they would try to slip off by themselves, I would stay right with them. I knew they didn't like that, but I didn't care.

After a little while, I said that I was going back to Georgia. Brenda hit the ceiling. She didn't like that at all. Her friend asked us to spend the night, and I told him no, that I had to go to work.

He said, "I can bring her home when I make a run down that way."

I said, "No way."

"My, my, you sound like Brenda is your girl," he said.

I looked at Brenda and said, "Do you want to tell him or should I?"

Brenda told him that we had been dating for a while.

I said, "I'm leaving, are you coming or staying?"

I found out later that they had dated in the past. Brenda wanted to stay, but she wanted to be with me too.

So, I said, "It's him or me, or the highway."

She looked at him and said, "Well, I had better go."

So, they said goodbye to each other and away we went. She didn't speak for a while.

I said, "Brenda, why don't you tell me about him."

She said, "I didn't want him to know about us."

"I guess you'll use to be lovers," I said.

She said, "It was a while ago—you can understand that, can't you?"

I said, "You should have told me about him and maybe I would understand better."

She told me she didn't know how she felt about him so I asked her if she wanted to go and stay with him for a while. She said, "I'm with you, ain't I?"

I said, "Isn't your mind back there with him? I don't want your mind there and your body here with me."

Then, she used that same old smile. When she got ready to make up, she knew how to get my mind off other things and back on her. Brenda had a way like no other girl. She knew how to calm me down. She would make you forget everything else, and she always got her way with me.

I was getting sleepy, so she slid over close to me and started kissing me. I told her to stop because I couldn't see where I was driving. She didn't care. When Brenda got ready to make up, you'd better just pull over. That is one of the things I liked about Brenda—she never stayed mad for long.

We were on our way back to Georgia. One of the things I miss about Brenda is that she would always ride with me and sit close to me with her arm around me. It makes you feel special. There were other girls who were prettier than Brenda, but not as sexy. I often wondered why I couldn't find someone like her to settle down with. She didn't drink alcohol, and neither did I when I was with her.

When we got back to Atlanta and back home to where I lived with my brother, I still had a week of vacation left, so I asked Brenda if she wanted to go to Florida.

She said, "Yes, let's go."

I told my brother goodbye, and off to LaGrange, Georgia we went. We went by to see my mom and dad and Carolyn. I thought it would be a good idea for her to meet Mom. When we got to Mom's house, I told her that Brenda and I were going to get married.

My sister, Carolyn, and Brenda hit it off from the start; they were a lot alike. I was in the kitchen talking to Mom and I looked out the window and saw Carolyn and Brenda. Brenda was strutting around in those yellow shorts. I thought to myself—there goes a girl who doesn't have a care in the world. She was so happy and it made me feel good to know she was happy.

We told Mom and Dad goodbye, and then we were on our way to Florida to see my brother Dick and his wife, Deedie. We decided to take Carolyn with us, so we went by to pick her up. Mama liked Brenda. Brenda had a way of making people like her.

Mama had asked me why I wanted to marry someone who already had two children. I told my mom to think back to when she and Dad were in love, and she would understand. I told her that I had never loved anyone the way I loved Brenda. I knew she was a flirt, but I never thought she meant any harm in it. I always liked making Brenda mad at me so we could make up. Each time, she would be sweeter and sweeter. She had a way of knowing how to love a man and to make him feel special.

When we got to Florida, Dick and I went fishing. When we got back, Deedie said Carolyn and Brenda had gone to the store. They later came back and were acting silly. I knew they had been drinking.

Brenda never drank much; she really didn't like it. She came over to me and tried to kiss me. I told her that she had been drinking. She said that she and Carolyn had gone to shoot pool and had drank a couple of beers. I asked her if they found any men, and Carolyn said no. I told her that was good—to just keep it fun between the girls. I wasn't worried about them having fun, but knew that when they were together, they could be bad.

We had a good time visiting with my brother and his family. Then, it was time to go back to Georgia. We stopped at Mom's house in LaGrange and left Carolyn. Then, it was back to Fayetteville, Georgia. We put off marriage and just kept a committed relationship. Then we broke up. It was the true love of my life—but the story isn't quite over yet.

I knew Brenda was getting restless and before long, she was gone. I also knew she would be back.

I didn't see her for a while. Then she showed up and told me she was marrying a soldier named Bill, who was stationed at Ft. McPherson. She put her arms around my neck and told me she only had a few weeks before he got back, and that she was all mine until then.

I told her she was like a ghost—you come for a while and then go. She asked me if she felt like a ghost when I held her, and I said no. I told her I didn't care if she was getting married—that I would always love her. She told me that just because she was getting married didn't mean she didn't love me. She said she would always love me and belong to me. She told me she didn't love Bill like she loved me, but that she needed to belong somewhere.

We were together for two weeks, and then she had to leave. I hated to see her go. Before she left, she told me she was going to have my baby. I kind of knew the baby was mine, but she married the soldier anyway.

I didn't marry her because she was pregnant. The soldier didn't know she was pregnant and that he would have a baby to care for. I knew Brenda could not be true to one man and that if I married her, she would run around on me. She would always come back to me and, like a dummy, I would always take her back. She had a spell on me—I guess it was love.

The next time I saw her was at one of my hang-outs, while I was having lunch with my brother. The owner of the restaurant asked me to guess who worked there. It rattled my brain, but I could not figure out who he meant. I asked who it was and he told me to wait and see. I turned around and saw Brenda. She was just standing there. We stood there looking at each other.

I stood up and said, "Come here, girl."

She ran to me and wrapped her arms around me and kissed me. We looked at each other for a while. Then, the owner said the drinks were on the house. One of the reasons I went to this club was for the good food.

It wasn't long before Brenda and her husband moved away. That was much better for me, but a month away from Brenda felt like a year. We both knew that sooner or later, our romance would have to end. He would get stationed somewhere else and they would move. But, as long as she was around, she was my girl.

Brenda was always here one day and gone the next. She would never be tamed by one man. I guess it wasn't meant to be. She broke my heart every time she ran off. When she came back, she mended the broken pieces for a while.

When I went to Brenda's mom's house for lunch sometime, I would see my daughter, Debbie. She was about five months old then. When I pulled up, Brenda would just stand there with a smile on her face. When she did that, she meant business. She was all woman and she knew it.

Her husband Bill did not bother me. He knew I was not afraid of him. I felt bad for him at times, because as long as she wanted me, that was the way it was going to be.

One day, Bill came in to the Dutch Kitchen where I hung out. I think he was hoping to catch Brenda and me together. Bill knew me, but he wasn't sure who was bringing her home at night. He was sitting on a bar stool so I went over and sat next to him. I told him hello and asked him why he was there.

Then, Brenda came from the kitchen and stood at the other end of the bar. She knew that I carried a gun, but she didn't know how brave Bill was. She stood and waited to see what would happen.

I hated that they were married—I wanted her free from him. To me, they had no business getting married, because Brenda did not belong to one man for long.

Bill knew Brenda was at the other end of the bar but did not look at her. He sat there like he didn't know her. I told him to look and see who was standing at the other end of the bar. He told me he saw her, but he didn't look her way.

I told Brenda to look and see who I was sitting with, and I asked her if he was her husband, and did she even know him. I told her that he was acting as though he didn't know who she was, and that if she were my wife, I would be loving on her right then. I told her to come down, and she did, and stood right by me.

I asked, "Brenda, do you know him? If you don't, then I want you to be mine."

Bill still wouldn't look at her. I pulled her close to me and gave her a kiss. She put her arms around my neck, and I told him that is how a husband should act.

She was loving it. I told her that she was acting like I was her husband, and that it felt good. I patted her and sent her on her way.

I told Bill that he knew I was the one picking her up from work and taking her home at night. I told him I knew he saw us kissing in the car. He told me that he thought so, but wasn't sure.

I said, "Are you sure now?"

He said, "Yes, I know it was you."

Brenda was just sitting and waiting to see what would happen. Larry, the owner, and Brenda, knew it wouldn't take much to set me off. She had never seen Bill put to a test like this.

I asked him how he could be so calm, knowing Brenda was going with me. He said that if it wasn't me, it would be someone else, and that she had told him about us. Bill told me he still loved her, and that I had better enjoy her while I could, because she would not be around for long.

I told him that Brenda would always come back to me and that it would take more than papers to hold her. He told me that when she wasn't with me, she was a different person. Then he said something to really set me off. He said, "You won't have her much longer; watch and see."

That did it. I grabbed him by the hair and pulled his head back. I asked him what he was talking about. Larry and Brenda came over. Brenda knew I had my pistol and had my hand on it. She asked me to let him go.

I asked Bill what he did in the Army—wash laundry. I told him he wasn't a man and he didn't say anything. I had his head pulled back and told him again that he wasn't a man. Brenda told me not to use my gun. I let him go and Brenda tried to talk to him, but he left and got in his car. Brenda ran back to me and put her arms around me. She told me she loved me and I told her I loved her too. Everyone in the bar clapped their hands and was happy for us.

I went to Brenda's mom's house to say our goodbyes, because she and Bill were leaving. I still was not expecting her to leave this way, but I would rather she leave with Bill than with a stranger. I didn't expect her to be with him long, and thought she would be back soon.

Here I was saying goodbye to the only girl I loved. Brenda was crying as I kissed the baby goodbye. Her family knew me and liked me a lot. Bill was her man for now, though.

He looked at her and asked her why she was crying. He looked at me and then told her to tell me goodbye.

She came over and gave me a kiss, and told me she didn't want to leave. I told her it wasn't the end of the world and it wasn't the end of her, and that I was not letting her go that easy. She told me that she loved me and she would see me in two weeks. That was the hardest thing I ever had to do.

Bill told her to let me go and come on. She went and got in the car and was really crying. Bill was happy though. He thought that because he was taking her far away, he had saved their marriage. He didn't know Brenda very well.

In two weeks, she was back at her mother's with my baby. She called me and told me she was back at her mom's. At lunch time, off I went, about five miles down the road. We were back together again. It seemed that there was nothing that could keep us apart. After a week, I got a call from Bill, at work.

He said, "James, you know that you can get in trouble going with a soldier's wife."

I said, "Hey, Bill, I can't help it if she wants me instead of you. Bill, I'm not going with her; she is going with me."

He said, "Call it what you like. I want you to bring her home because the kids need her. She hired a babysitter until I get home every day. Now, that is her job, to watch the kids."

I said, "Bill, you can't hold her. If it wasn't me, it would be someone else. Why don't you get a divorce? Your problems would be over and they would then be my problems. What do you think?"

He said, "James, I want you to bring her home, and I won't have you locked up when you get here. Just drop her off and leave. That's all you have to do. If you don't, I am coming up there and bringing my gun with me."

I said, "Bill, now you know better than to threaten me. If you want to come up, then come on. I will be waiting for you."

Then I got to thinking about it. I had been out there in Ft. McPherson when I was AWOL in 1954. So, I did not want any trouble with the MPs.

I told Brenda that she needed to go back and take care of her kids, because they were hers too. I talked her into it, but it wasn't easy. We both knew it would end sooner or later, but right then, Brenda was hung up on me.

So, I took her to Savannah and let her off two blocks from the house. She cried all the way there. When she got out of the car, she kept kissing me and saying how much she loved me. I told her I loved her too. I told her that she had to go, and for her to not look back, because if she did, I would have to take her home with me.

She had left the baby with her mom. As she walked away, it was more than I could bear. It was hard to let her go. Soon, we would have to put our love aside and go on with our lives.

She wrote me and called often. I would go down to her mom's house and eat lunch often. I would play with my daughter and hold her. It was hard to let her go, but as they say, "all good things must come to an end".

She called me one day and told me she was going to her mother's, and I couldn't wait to get there. When I drove up, she was waiting for me, and she came running to the car when it came to a stop.

Now, we had two weeks together before I would take her home again. Those two weeks was just like it was when we first met. We were together all the time. We never let each other out of sight. We stayed close together all the time. Brenda was always looking over her shoulder, as if someone or something was after her.

I can truly say that Brenda could never settle down with one man, because she was always looking a far off. Now, why was she like that? I will never know. When we were together, as far as we were concerned, the world could just pass us by.

I remember, at night, I would always hold her tight while she was sleeping, and if I let her go for just a minute, she would always start to reach for me. Yes, I can truly say that Brenda would never belong to just one man—she belongs to the world. I now know that you can still love somebody and still have other loves in your life. I am not saying that it's right, but that's the way love is.

She was mine for a season, someone else's tomorrow. I knew then that our love would have to come to an end. Now, I did have other girlfriends when Brenda was not around. When she'd come back to be in my life, I would tell the one I was going with about Brenda, and that I'd have to spend time with her while she was around. I would call the other girls when she would leave.

Now, that's the way it was with me and Brenda. We had that special kind of love for each other. When she was around, it was like no one else mattered at all. All that seemed to matter was that we would be together for a little while.

I know y'all have seen people like that. I don't know, but it's just like when she was around, nothing seemed to matter. She had such a hold on me.

I also know, if the other girl named Joyce had left her boy-friend and wanted to come back, I'd have to take her back. She was my girlfriend at age sixteen. I spoke about her prior to this chapter. Even now, when I think about her, I fall in love with her all over again. She was very special.

Back then, when a man loved a woman, it meant something. When we fell in love, we didn't stop and stare at every other girl that came along. Our love for that person meant something—at least, that's the way it was with me.

I loved both Brenda and Joyce, but Brenda was altogether different from Joyce. I guess you would have called Brenda a "red-neck". She was the kind of girl that would jump on you in a minute.

Joyce was the quiet type. I still miss that girl. I also miss what Brenda and I had.

When Brenda was with me, it was as though we were mar-ried. I couldn't keep my hands off of her. She was the same way with me. I guess what I liked about Brenda was that when we'd ride together in the car, she would always sit up close to me, with her arms around my neck, no matter where we were or where we went. I loved her for that.

Now days, when you see a couple, they are not sitting close like that. All couples seem to act the way older couples do, now.

Now, we were both wrong for the way we did, but what can I say? Was it love or just affection for each other?

I had a friend, or a buddy of mine, and we'd go to the bars and drink beers together, and shoot pool together, too. This friend had a beautiful sister. She had long black hair. We met and she couldn't wait for me to ask her for a date.

She was about ten years younger than me. He name was Doris. When Brenda wasn't around, Doris was. We were together all the time. Now, she didn't love me, but she said she just wanted to be with me. That's the way it was with Doris and me. She wanted me and I wanted her.

With Brenda, it was different. When she was around we could feel the fire inside of us for each other.

Now, Doris was a beautiful girl, but she just didn't have that fire in her like Brenda. Brenda and I shared our love for each other as much as we could. Brenda was being pulled one way and then the other. I think she liked it that way. There was one thing about Brenda, when she was around me there was never a dull moment. She was so full of that special kind of love. We had a lot of good times together, and we also shared a lot of love together. It was as if we knew that it would be our last time together. It was hard for me to let her go, but we both knew that time was running out, so we spent as much time as we could together. The time came for us to say our goodbyes, and she held on to me as if she would never see me again.

We played with the baby for a while, and then I had to take her home. I didn't see them for a long time after that, but I did still love them.

I had not seen them for three years, and by this time, Brenda and Bill were divorced. Bill kept the boys, and Brenda kept Debbie. By this time, I had just about gotten over her.

One day, while I was working, I got a call and it was Brenda. She told me she was in Santa Barbara, California. I asked her what she was doing and she told me that she and Bill had divorced.

She told me that she and Debbie were coming home in a few weeks. She told me that Debbie was three, and still didn't know who her daddy was. I told her she should tell her and Brenda said she did not want to. She was afraid I would take Debbie, and that she was all Brenda had to remember me by.

I told her she didn't have to go all the way out to California and that she could come home. She said she didn't want to put me through that. By this time, she had been out of my life for a while, and I was married and had a son. He was one year old, but my wife and I didn't get along too well. But I told Brenda we were going to stay together for the sake of my son.

When Brenda got home, she called me and I went to pick her up. She was not as young, but still had that thing about her. She didn't have Debbie with her. We hugged and said hello. I still felt the same way for her. I figured that if you still felt that way after three years, it had to be love.

Brenda and I were back together for a while. Brenda had not changed much. She still couldn't keep still, and she lived each day as if it were her last. I knew she was not going to be around for long. She acted as though she knew there was something out there for her. I couldn't reach her anymore.

We both knew it was a matter of time before she would be gone out of my life again. Every time she left, she took a part of me with her. I could see her running in a field of clover with her hair blowing in the wind and her arms outstretched with a big smile on her face. She was like a wild horse that could not be tamed. I guess that is what made her so special.

Again, she left and it broke my heart. I had no idea where she went, but I knew wherever she was, I still loved her.

I will never forget her. She was mine even if it was only for a season.

So I said, "Goodbye, my love. I will never forget you. For as long as I live, you will have a part of me.

"I can still see you standing there in the door with that smile on your face. I can see you running in the wind with your hair blowing and a smile on your face. I can see you coming into my life and I can see you leaving me all over again. I will look for you everywhere I go. I can truly say that the years we had together were the greatest times of my life.

"Brenda, through all the years I have known you, I have loved you. So, dear, if we never love again, I can truly say that I have known one true love. If everyone could have one love in their life like I did, they can say they have known love.

"I don't know if I can ever love anyone again the way I loved you or if I have any love left for anyone else. Now, as I look, I can still see your arms around my neck. I can still see you leaving and then turning around and waving goodbye to me while crying. I wish we could turn back the hands of time. But you know, Brenda, it was you who always walked away. But that does not matter. I was always glad to see you come back, even if it was only for a little while.

"Remember, my love, I will always love you. You were special to me. So, goodbye my love. I will miss you very much and I still love you very much."

This story is true. I should know, because it happened to me.

8

Finding My Daughter after Forty Years

Brenda was gone again. I didn't hear from her for years. I would hear, from time to time, that she was in a certain place. Sometimes I would ride around in different towns to see if I could find her. I had been alone, now, for a long time. One day, someone told me that she lived somewhere down below Griffin.

I was always riding around in different towns looking for old cars for my son and me to restore and sell. Once, I was riding through a mobile home park and saw a woman standing in the door. I slammed on my brakes, because she looked like Brenda. I guess the woman thought I was crazy, because she was not Brenda.

I lived in Hampton, Georgia around 1990. One day she called me. A mutual friend had given her my number, and she asked if she could come over. I was so excited to hear from her so, of course, I wanted her to come over. I told her that would be fine. She had been in a car wreck and had broken her leg. She also had put on a few pounds since I had seen her, but other than that, she was in good shape.

When she arrived, I looked out the door and saw her coming up, walking on crutches. She had broken her ankle. Here we were once again.

We said hello to one another and sat down so we could begin to catch up on our lives. We talked and we went back in time for a little while. She had put on a few pounds, like I said, and she was a little heavy, but it was nothing that I couldn't deal with. It was still hard for me to keep my hands to myself, but we both knew it was no good, because we had been down that road before.

It was great to see her. I have wished many times that we could have spent our lives together, but that would have been hard to do. She was just a free spirit. When she started to leave, we hugged one another and said goodbye. There were tears shed—tears that will never be settled.

The next time I saw Brenda was in a church about three miles from where I lived. I attended church there, and they let me sing sometimes. Brenda had changed a lot since the last time I saw her. But, I thought, who hasn't? I finally talked to her and she wanted to come and visit me sometime. I told her that she was welcome to come. It had been fifteen years (in 1990) since I had seen Brenda.

She came to see me. She sat down and we talked, and we spent some time reliving our past, but that was many years ago. I got out my guitar and we sang several songs together. I still remember all the good times we had together. I also understand that is all in the past now.

She had told her mom and sisters that she felt as though I didn't like her anymore because of her weight. I guess she felt like that because I had said, "Brenda, you attracted me years ago by keeping yourself trimmed down." I had told her that it was her fault, and had asked her why couldn't she get back to the size she was. I knew that could never happen and things could never be like they were in the past. After she left, we didn't see each other much. I stay busy with my music and singing.

Brenda and I had a daughter together. She is now forty years old and her name is Debbie. I asked Brenda if she thought it was about time for her to let me know where she lived. Finally she agreed to let me know all the details.

Brenda told me that she lived in Georgia. I talked Brenda into taking me down there. So, we took a trip so I could see my daughter for the first time since she was a baby. I was very uptight. It was about 130 miles from where I lived in Fayetteville, Georgia. All I could say was, "Brenda, how could you cause my daughter and me to be apart for so long?"

We finally reached our destination. Brenda and I got out of the car and went inside. We sat down, but my daughter was not home at that time. She came in a little later.

Brenda told her that I was her dad. She pointed to a man sitting across the room that had raised her and said, "That is my dad sitting over there. He is the only dad I have ever known." Then she sat down in the floor and started playing with the kids.

Debbie had been married, but her husband had died. She has one son and one daughter; the son is 21 and the daughter is 19. Her son has a little girl who is two and one-half years old. Her daughter has a little boy who is seven months old.

"I'm going out on the front porch to smoke," she said.

I asked her if it would be okay if I came along with her. She said, "Okay, it's fine with me; you can do what you want to do."

When we got outside, she and I talked. I just let her say what she wanted to say first. She really got it all out, too, and she was doing a lot of crying.

She finally looked at me and said, "Didn't you even one time want to know where I was?"

I told her that I had not heard from Brenda for 15 years, and that she had left me and she was hard to find. I told her I should have tried to see her when she was younger, but that I was so wrapped up in her mother. I also told her that I was sorry.

She looked at me and said, "Well, Dad, it's not your fault, and I don't blame you. Mom knew where you were all that time and she could have told me where you were."

"It feels funny to call you Dad," she said.

We agreed that we would keep in touch from that point on, and we would never lose touch again. I told her about her brother, my son, and that he was 38 years old. She told me that she wanted to meet him and she was excited about that. She was so shocked that her mother had kept her from her dad and brother all those years because she could have been growing up with a dad and brother. She said that if that had happened, she may not have had to go through the things she did growing up.

The following Christmas she wanted to come up and spend a little time with us. My brother and I went down to get her, and we brought her back to Fayetteville to spend some time with us. She finally got to meet her brother and my sister. We took a lot of pictures.

My son seemed really glad to have a sister and have a chance to meet her. I believe it would have been a lot better if they had had the chance to grow up knowing one another. We all went out to eat, and then we went Christmas shopping. It felt a little strange. I had not seen my daughter since she was a baby, and here we were, shopping together for the first time.

But, we finally got a chance to meet and exchange phone numbers, so we don't have to worry about losing each other again. I had seen this kind of thing on TV and didn't think it would ever happen to me.

When I look back, I feel that I should have taken the time to find her and not waited on Brenda. Now that we all know about each other, we can get together whenever we want. We cannot go back in time and change things, but we can start where we are and make a future together.

9

My Son and His Family

I'd like to tell you about my son and his family. My son's name is James Beckom, Jr. His wife's name is Anita. They have three daughters—Tiffany, Tori and Tabitha. All of the girls are very pretty.

Tiffany is the oldest, at 19, and attends Georgia State University. I was talking to Tiffany about college and she said that she was not going to party, but to study. That made me feel a lot better about her.

Tori is the middle child, and is 16 years old. She just got her first car and she was so happy when she got it. I remember letting her drive my 4-door Chevy truck. I must say she drove it better than I did, mainly because she is so tall and could see out the windows better. She has two more years before she goes to college.

Tabitha is the youngest of the three, at age nine. She loves to play and has a lot of energy. She is the apple of her parents' eye, as well as mine.

My son has his own business and is successful. Forty-five years ago I began dealing and working on cars. At the age of 13, my son began to help me. As a result of that, his hobby is buying older cars, restoring them, and selling them. He works very hard to take care of his family and give them everything they need.

His wife, Anita, keeps the house and takes care of the girls, which is a big job. I am very proud of my son and his family.

Everyone who knows my son tells me what a fine person he is. If I ever need anything, I know he will always be there for me.

10

Deaths in the Beckom Family

I would like to tell you about the deaths in my immediate family. There were 13 children in our family—eight boys and five girls. My father died in 1973 of a stroke, and my mother died in 1995.

My oldest brother, Milt, was married and had one child. He died of a cerebral hemorrhage in 1981.

My youngest brother, Larry, was married and had four children. He divorced and later married again and they had two children. He was in a horrible automobile accident in 1986, and laid in a coma for 15 months before he died.

My brother, Tommy, married and had one child. He then divorced and later married again. He had four children with his second wife. He developed colon cancer and died from that in 1990.

My brother, Dick, had three sons by his first marriage and none by his second marriage. He died of pancreatic cancer in 2000.

The last one to die in my family was my sister Carolyn, in 2006. She was in the hospital with bronchitis and died of a pulmonary embolism.

My brother, Perry, had four boys and one girl. Two of his sons have died.

My sister, Mary Ann, had one boy and two girls. One of her daughters died in 1994.

My oldest sister, Ida, lives in Atlanta. Her husband is dead. She has three boys and two grandchildren. Ida is retired, but spends her time volunteering at churches helping others.

I have a brother named Bobby, who lives in LaGrange. He is retired and sits around taking it easy.

I have a sister named Janelle. She is married, has one child and one grandson. She lives in Winterville, Georgia. She is now a retired housewife, but she is also involved in the ministry.

My youngest sister, Cathy, is not married. She lives in Marietta, Georgia. She has been serving the Lord since she was seven years old. I do not know how she has done it, but I sure am proud of her.

I have a brother named Jack. I saved him for last because he is the youngest and I am proud of him. He has made a very good life for himself. He and his wife, Carla, live on a farm called Twin Dreams Farm in Barnesville, Georgia. They raise cattle and horses. They have show horses, and the horses have won several ribbons for them. They have four children between them. Jack has three grandchildren. God has really blessed Jack and Carla because they are giving people. Our family goes to their farm for gatherings often.

I know that I shamed my family when I got into trouble, and I am sorry for that. I know they have forgiven me.

I have told you about my family and the deaths to show that life has been hard on our family. I do believe that all of those who have died were ready to go and are with the Lord. I also thought you might be interested in knowing about my family. There are four boys and four girls still living in our family.

11

Carolyn's Funeral

There are many people in the world who have lost loved ones, and they don't know how to deal with the pain. Because they don't have God in their lives, they don't have a clear understanding of why people leave this earth.

I remember when we lost our mother. At the time, I was out of the will of God and felt as though I just could not handle it. I have learned since that I need the fellowship of the church and having them to support you. So, when Mom died, it was hard to deal with. When someone close to you dies, you need the relationship with God to get you through it. The kind of love that God can give you is the love that can heal you.

On February 22, 2006, we lost our sister Carolyn. She was a special kind of person. A few years ago, Carolyn and I could never get along. She always wanted the last word and so did I.

Later on, I got sick with cancer and God healed me. He sent me out on a mission for Him. I was back in church, singing for God and making tapes. I gave Carolyn my tapes and I would talk to her about the Lord, which was also on my tapes.

I remember before she died, she would tell me, "Hey, James, you sound like a preacher on those tapes. Don't you ever stop singing and talking about God; you are good, now."

After I got closer to Carolyn, I got to know her in a different way. We stopped arguing so much and I began to understand her a lot better. You see, it was God who showed me who she was. That's the way it is with God. He helps you to see things clearly. The closer you get to Him, the better understanding you will have about a lot of things in life.

When my sister died, I did not have to shed a tear, and I will tell you why. Carolyn did not want a sad funeral, but every funeral I had ever been to was sad. That was until we had her funeral. The man from the funeral home said that he had never been to a funeral like hers. He said this one felt more like a home coming. We gave her the kind of funeral she wanted.

Janelle started it off. She let everyone that wanted to speak about our sister do just that. She had a lot of nieces and nephews, and they were all crazy about her. We laughed a lot at her funeral. Some of us were even praising the Lord. My brother Perry said a few words and read a scripture. I sang a song.

Carolyn had told me that she loved the song, "Where the Roses Never Fade." So, after I talked, I sang that song. My brother Jack said I was going to make him cry. I told him to just think about it—she was gone to a land where the roses never faded. Isn't that great?

Then, my sister Cathy read a scripture and ended it with prayer. I know Carolyn would have been pleased with her funeral. Very few tears were shed. Remember, Jesus said, "Weep not for the dead, but weep for the living." You see, my sister has gone on to a better place now and is much better off. I know in my heart that she is with our mom and dad, Tommy, Larry,

Dick and Milt. She is also with her daughter, Gina. Gina died at the age of twelve.

The best advice I can give you is to make sure that you know Christ. Make sure you are ready. Don't give any room to the devil to use you and get you where he wants you. We will all see my sister again some day if we keep living for the lord.

12

A Farmer and the Preacher Man

This is a short story about a farmer. It reminds me of some of the good old times I had on the farm.

I asked this old timer named Bill how he was doing. He kind of dropped his head and then he told me that his wife and kids had been sick. He said that he had been down with the flu, and his cows were dry. "But," he said, "we are still living, so I guess everything is okay."

He said that his hens would not lay any eggs. The hogs took the colic and they all got sick and died. The bees got mad and left their hives. Weevils got into the corn and the rain rotted all the hay. Then, he said, "We are still living so everything is okay."

The porch rotted down, causing more expenses. The mule tore down the fences. The mortgage was due and there was no money to pay it. The cow broke into the field and ate all the peas. The rabbits got all the tomatoes, and his mother-in-law had just come to live with them. Then he said, "We are still living, so everything is all right."

He said, "My land is so poor and dry; it is yellow and beginning to crack open." Then he said, "We are still living, so everything is okay."

The well had gone dry so I have to carry the water up from the spring that is about a mile and a quarter away. The house leaks when it rains and everything we have gets wet. The chimney fell down just the other day. Then he said, "We are still living, so everything is okay."

The corn meal is gone and we have run out of meat. I have nothing to kill to put in the smoke house. The preacher is coming Sunday to spend the day. But, "We are still living, so everything is okay."

The canned stuff spilled and jars got broken. We are going to have a new baby around the first of May. My crops rotted in the ground. I asked the bank for a loan and they turned me down. But, "We are still living so everything is okay."

I don't know what we are going to feed the preacher on Sunday. All we have left is one old Billy goat and I bet he is so tough that we will have to take a saw and cut him up so we can eat him. I do not know what else could possibly go wrong. If I didn't have bad luck, I would have no luck at all. But, "We are still living, so everything is okay."

I asked the preacher, "Preacher man, when are things going to get better?"

He said, "Well, I just don't know but if the next meal is like the last one, you had better take it to the corn mill and have it ground up so you can eat it."

The preacher man said, "Hey, Bill, you don't have another one of those billy goats, do you? I was just thinking that I could grind it up and it would make good hamburgers."

Bill told the preacher that he had never thought about that and that it was a good idea. There we were using a saw to cut it up and it was as tough as leather. The preacher man said, "Hey, Bill, next time you kill a goat, grind it up and make it into hamburger meat, and some stew too."

I said, "Hey, preacher, why didn't I think of that?"

By then, Bill said, my stomach was growling so loud I couldn't think straight. I asked the preacher when he was going to have that dinner on the ground because my stomach was growling and I knew my wife was hungry too.

The preacher told me he knew some people who had goats that were too old to mate and they put them out in a pasture and retired them. He said he bet they wouldn't even miss one or two every now and then. The preacher said, "Let's go get one and we can grind it up and make some stew. Your family wouldn't know the difference between cow and goat stew."

Bill asked the preacher what they were going to do when the man ran out of goats. Preacher said, "Well, we'll just have to ask the good Lord if we can start on the sheep; one time we can get a goat, the next time we can get a sheep. That way, he won't miss them as quickly."

Bill asked, "Preacher, ain't that stealing?"

Preacher said, "We don't call it stealing; we call it feeding the stomach. Besides, you know you have to have milk for the baby when it arrives. So, that means you will need to sell a little to get money to buy the baby some milk. People won't know the difference between goats and cows."

Bill asked if that was right to do.

The preacher said, "Well, you know what they say—you've got to get the ox out of the ditch."

Bill said, "Preacher, you know you are all right, but don't they pay you at the church?"

The preacher said most of the people were like Bill—their crops had dried up and they didn't have any money. The preacher said he wondered what they were doing for food.

Bill said, "You don't think they are doing the same thing we are doing, do you?"

Preacher said, "Well if they are, these goats and sheep aren't going to last long. I'll tell you, Bill, I am kind of tired of these goats and sheep anyway. Why don't we leave these goats and sheep alone and start borrowing a cow because they will make us a lot more steaks and beef stew."

Bill said to the preacher, "When you first came here, I thought you were one of those snooty preachers but you turned out to be an all right guy. The Lord always said that He would provide for His own. Doesn't it say in the Bible that the righteous would never be forsaken or go hungry? You know preacher, there is nothing left here but a lot of poor people. We all work on halves with the wealthy. Say, preacher, do you think that God sent you here to feed the hungry? I don't know much about the Bible, but you are a preacher. There are all kinds of preachers. Some get rich off of the poor and others just go along with the poor. No one had better talk about you to me because, in my book, you are all right."

The preacher said, "Well, Bill, I sure hope the Lord feels the same way."

Bill said, "Well, somebody had to show us how to feed our family. After the bank turned me down, the rich owner would not help us either. We were about to starve and God sent the preacher. Now if that wasn't a miracle, I don't know what else it could have been."

Bill said that the crops were doing better. Instead of the rabbits eating up the garden, they were eating the rabbits. He said he didn't know what they would do when all the rabbits were gone. He said they had to stop eating the man's goats, sheep and cattle. They were thinning out pretty quickly. He said the preacher still came every Sunday for dinner. He said the last Sunday they didn't have rabbit, they had t-bone steaks instead. After all, he said, one cow every now and then wouldn't be missed too much. He said if things got too bad, there was always another farm somewhere else.

He said that he and his family had gotten closer to the preacher, that he was like a part of the family. He said they got the old place fixed up and preacher was still coming over every Sunday. He said the preacher was still preaching, and his family was still growing. He said the preacher is still single and looking for a wife.

Bill said he hoped it didn't take long, that the preacher was a good man and deserved a good wife. He said that if his family kept growing, it would be as big as Abraham's and he would have to build a bigger house. He said he wasn't complaining. He said things were going well at the farm, and thanks to the preacher, his mother-in-law was still there and he had a lot of help on the farm.

Bill said that late in the evening he and his wife would sit on the front porch in the swing and hold hands while looking at their big family and thank God for it.

Then Bill said, "Goodbye, and thank you, Lord, for sending the preacher man by this way.

13

Think Before You Speak

This is a story about a lady down the street. You will find these kinds of people everywhere. It may be your next-door neighbor. These people talk too much. Be careful what you say about people, because a loose tongue can cause a lot of damage. Don't be a tale bearer. Think before you talk about someone else, because it could be a close friend that you hurt.

The tongue can carry bad news. The tongue that carries bad seeds will leave bad seeds everywhere it goes, unless you make no mistakes in your life.

A neighbor was passing by my garden one day and she stopped and looked at me. I knew she was stopping to gossip and not to look at my flowers. This is what she said: "You know, that girl down the street should be run out of our neighborhood. She drinks and does a lot of talking. She shouldn't be allowed to wander up and down these streets. She is a tale bearer. When I see her, I cross over to the other side of the street. She knows better than to talk to me and my little girl. I don't have anything to do with her because she is a bad person." Then she looked at me, smiled and said goodbye.

She went on to the next neighbor who was standing outside. I thought to myself that she just did not know how bad she sounded.

The Bible says that the tongue is a hard thing to tame. The tongue has even broken up marriages. It is all because people can't seem to be able to control their tongues. This particular part of our body can get more people in trouble. I thought that if my neighbor only knew that she would have to eat those bad words that she had spoken, perhaps she wouldn't have opened her mouth and spilled the negativity.

People with loose tongues have more on their minds than God. Godly people do not gossip that way. The Holy Spirit who lives inside of you won't let negativity come from your lips. If you have a loose tongue, be careful of the stones that you throw. It could be a friend down the street that you hit. Now take heed to this part of the story.

While my neighbor was gossiping about that poor girl down the street, she heard a speeding car coming down the road. Next, there was a squealing of tires and screeching of brakes. It was a sound that made my blood chill. It made me weak all over. It was the sound of death.

The next thing you know, my neighbor's daughter was seen being pulled from underneath the same car that had just come to a screeching halt. The lady that pulled her from underneath the car did not make it. The neighbor who does so much gossiping began running down the street to where she heard the noise. She saw the little girl standing there with all the other bystanders. They were looking down at the broken body of the lady who had pulled the little girl from the car. She grabbed her daughter and hugged her as tight as she could.

Then she said, "Who was that dear lady who saved my little girl and lies there all broken up?"

I told her that the lady was the same lady she had been speaking badly about earlier and that she saved her daughter. You never know, but the one you carry tales about may be the one who saves you one day. God can turn things around on you in a second in an attempt to save you from your sin before it is too late.

We need to learn how to control our tongues. I don't know if my neighbor has learned her lesson or not from that incident. I do know, though, that she will have plenty of time to think about it.

I know there are a lot of people who don't work and spend their time on the telephone all day talking to other people. I have listened to preachers preach about the tongue. My brother Larry even preached about it when he was still living. People will always listen to the word but they never receive it.

I have learned not to listen to the tale bearer. You see, it helps no one. Remember this every time you talk about someone else: unless it is to help them, don't do it. If you cannot find anything else to do with your life, pick up the Bible and read it. You will find a lot more peace of mind there than in talking about others. Think of this and remember it whether you are a Christian or not. God hears every word you speak. Ask the Lord to help you to say nice things about others or say nothing at all. Train your tongue and be in charge of the words it delivers to listeners.

I used to talk about people myself, but the most important thing is that I learned and now I know better. I try my best to keep nothing but fruitful words flowing from my mouth. I want the respect of God and those around me. I don't want to be known as the guy that gossips and spreads fruitless words.

So, I ask all of my readers to please be careful of the stones that you throw. Be careful and don't sow your seeds in bad soil. Remember that our words are powerful weapons. They can be of help or harm, so make yours be of help and you will always have God blessing your life and your loved ones.

14

A Divorce Can Damage a Child's Mind

A little girl was praying at the close of the day because her daddy had gone away. On her little face was a look of despair. As I stood there listening, I was thinking of how sad this must be.

This little girl said, "Mama said daddy had brought us to shame and that I am never to mention his name again."

The little girl prayed and said, "Oh, Lord, take me. Help me to understand. And, Oh, Lord, please hold on to my hand so I will not stumble."

Now, I would like to tell you a story of a family that I once knew. We will just call them, Mary, Bill and Sue. Mary was a plain housewife. Bill was a business man, but a plain guy. It seemed as though he was standing still and never getting any-where. Sue was a beautiful girl. She went to school, loved to play and loved her mom and dad.

Now, Mary and Bill had their ups and downs, but it never amounted to anything. Neither one got mad. Then one day something happened and one word led to another, and then to a divorce. Now, here are two adults who failed to use common sense and were thinking only of themselves. They never stopped to think about the one that mattered the most—Sue. She did not ask to be in this situation.

Jesus said to "… train up a child in the way it should go." You have failed God as a man or women when you fail to teach your children about God and when you divorce.

My son was brought up in the Lord and knows that living in the will of God is the only right way to live. Do you pray for your child and talk about Jesus in your home? Do you take your child to church and let them go to Sunday school? Do you just lie at home in the bed and let the days pass by without teaching them the ways of God? You may not know it, but God will hold you responsible for what your child does until he or she becomes of age. When you divorce, you never stop to consider the one that will be hurt the most—the children. This world would be a better place if people thought more of others than themselves.

Mary and Bill hurt their little girl Sue. She said, "Lord, take me, hold my hand and lead me on the right path. And, Oh Heavenly Father, help me to understand why my mom and dad are getting a divorce. Lord, I thought that Mom and Dad told you that they would love each other until death. Lord, I do not understand why they do not love each other anymore. Lord, please make my mom and dad love each other again, because I love them both and I don't want them to get a divorce. Please, God, help me!"

A divorce sometimes can hurt just as bad as anything. It is always the children that get hurt. Times have changed so much since my mom and dad got married. When they said their vows, that was it. They lived together until death. Now marriages may last a few years and then people leave each other.

A house divided and without God cannot stand for long. Trying to have a marriage without consulting God first is a big mistake, and you are only setting yourself up for failure. It is like building a house on a bed of sand, which will eventually wash away. If you build your marriage on a solid foundation, it will stand the test of time and can endure all things.

Remember that when you get a divorce, it is always the children who get hurt. Not many people call upon God when they have trouble in their marriage. If they did, the divorce rate would not be so high.

I hope anyone reading this book who is having trouble in their marriage will think about the things I am saying and try to work out their problems with God and their themselves, especially if they have children. Children should not have to choose between their mom and dad. Remember the vows that you made in front of God and to each other. Settle down and raise your kids the proper way. Put your trust in God and He will help you find your way.

Don't rush into marriage because you are tricked by a nice smile or worldly possessions. Don't look at your problems with a carnal mind. If you have a good man and he provides for you and your family, then you are blessed beyond measure. You should thank God for sending you such a man.

If you have a good woman who takes care of the home, then you are blessed and should also thank God.

Feelings (emotions) may change as time passes, but that does not mean that you should give up on your marriage. Fight for your marriage and keep praying about it. Do not throw away your marriage and your family life for your own selfish reasons. Don't just look at each other's flaws, but try to find the good things about each other. Work on your flaws together. Bring healing to your marriage and keep your family together. Don't let your marriage go without fighting for it.

I know a family that went through a divorce. The wife divorced the husband. Later, he prospered and had great wealth. She wanted him back then, but it was too late.

Good men and good women are hard to find. When God blesses you with someone who will love you as you are, be thankful. Remember also that your children's happiness is at stake, and try not to be selfish in your final decision. Choosing a life partner without consulting God first is like building on that bed of sand. It may last for a while, but as soon as the rain comes, it will crumble. So, my friend, put your trust and your marriage in the hands of God. Remember your blessings and your children. Remember also that if the good outweighs the bad, then keep fighting. Also, the battle is not yours, but the Lord's. Give it to Him.

I hope this story will help some family that may be going through a trying time in their marriage.

15

A Mother's Love for Her Children

I had a dream about my mother last night.

When I was a little boy, Mom would always read me her Bible. How I still long for those days once more. You know, mothers always put their arms around you and smother you with their love and compassion. That's their way of showing you how much they love you.

As we grew older and would go out at night, Mama would never go to bed or close her eyes before we got home and we were safe in bed. She would sit up and read her Bible as she waited for us. Back then, we never thought much about it, though, because we were so young and restless and wild (at least most of us were, anyway). Mothers worry about their children—both now and back then.

Mom would lie in bed and listen as each one of us came home from being out or at work. She would hear the turning of the door knob, and as we entered the hall, she would call out our names to be sure of who was arriving. She did not have to worry about the girls as much as the boys. One of the boys lived a different life than the other boys. He became a preacher.

Mom would pray after she knew that each of us was home safe. Her prayer sounded something like this: "Lord, I thank you for bringing all my children home safely tonight." Mom would tell us all goodnight and then she would say to us, "When you are all grown and have children of your own, then and only then will you understand."

We all grew up and went our separate ways. Some of us went into the Armed Forces and others became businessmen and women. Some got married and had children.

One day we were all called in because our mother had taken ill. We gathered around her bed. She was going fast. With the last breath of strength she had left, she looked at us all and gave us the sweetest smile. It let us all know that everything was okay. Then she prayed that God would keep her children safe from harm through all of their lives; then she went to sleep. I feel she is waiting for us up in heaven. I'll see Mom, Dad and all my other loved ones there.

My friends, if you still have your mom and dad, please go visit them while they are still living. Learn to appreciate them more than you ever have. Love and respect them. You only get one set of parents, and after they are gone, it will be too late to try to express your feelings for them.

I've just been to heaven. You see, I dreamed about Mama last night. This is really a true story. It happens to every family.

16

Is Life Fair to Everyone? Maybe Not

As you travel through life, you will find many people who have fallen by the wayside. You will find them walking down the streets in any big city, or sitting in a bar. You will find them sitting in a park. You will find them in an alley behind a building. They are all over the world.

These are people who have gotten caught on the wrong side of the track. Some of them are homeless, and most are hopeless. Sometimes, when you fall so low, it takes someone else to lift you back up. Some of these people never get back up. They have become content with their lifestyle and they feel as though there is no way out. Some will allow you to help them, and some will turn your away.

I have a friend who is this way. He has gotten caught in the trap of being an alcoholic. He starts his day off by drinking. He will get drunk and then sleep it off. He wakes up the next day and starts it all over again. He says he is happy, but I don't think he is. How could he be happy unless he just does not feel there is any hope for him?

One day, I was going to a restaurant to eat. While driving down the road, I saw a man and a little girl. He was clean and neat but was holding a sign that read, "Down on my luck. Please help us." That little girl was about seven or eight years old, and was beautiful with long brown hair. It was in July, and the temperature was about 90 degrees. I honked my horn at them and the little girl came running over to me. I handed her a $20 bill. She thanked me and then ran back to her dad.

There were many people driving by in cars. If each of them had given just one dollar, they would have had enough money to maybe make a new start. I thought to myself that the little girl could be my granddaughter, but the grace of God kept that from happening. It could have been one of you also. But for the grace of God, it could be any of us. I went back by there to see if they needed a place to stay for the night, but they were gone.

You will meet many people like this in life. Open your heart to them. We do not have the right to judge or criticize. We should be as loving and kind as Christ was. To those who weep, death comes cheap—these men with broken hearts. So humbled we should be when they come passing by. Some lose faith and some lose love, where sorrow shoots her darts. With all hope gone, they walk alone—these men with broken hearts.

Life can be so cruel that the heart will pray for death. God, why must the living dead know pain with every breath? So, help your brother along the way. For the God we serve made them, just as He made you—these people with broken hearts. Be aware of other people. When you help someone else, you can go home and rest easy, knowing the joy you have brought into someone else's life.

I have helped many people. One time, I picked up a man in Riverdale and took him eighty miles down the road. I feel for these people because I have been in this position myself.

I saw a man once on the side of a road; I gave him half of the money I had. I don't know if he bought beer or wine with the money, but I prayed that God would watch over him and help him use the money wisely. I obeyed what my spirit was telling me to do.

If the Spirit tells you to help someone, then you should obey. Obey the Lord and He will let you live a good, long and abundant life. When you have done that, you can be in peace as you look back at your life. That's how I want to be in my last days—in peace—not worried about how much money you have or don't have, and just knowing that God's love is enough.

I read this story once, and want to share it with you.

A woman was cooking dinner for Jesus, and a man came and knocked on the door. She opened the door and he told her that he was hungry, and he wanted to know if she had food to spare. She told him to go away—that the food she had was for Jesus.

Another knock came and she answered, but this time she was angry. When she opened the door, she told him to go away and that she did not have any food for him.

Another knock came and she was really getting ready to let him have it this time. But this time, Jesus stood at her door.

She told him to come in and that dinner was ready. Jesus replied to her by saying, "No, it is not. For I have been here two times, and you said to go away, that the food was for Jesus only."

She was shocked and she asked him when had he been there? He told her that when she turned away a hungry man, she was turning Him away too.

So, my friend, remember to help your brother the next time you see someone in trouble. Turning away your brother is like turning God away. When you see someone in trouble, don't turn your head and walk on by. If you can help them, please do.

Know also that it does not always take material things to be of assistance. A simple prayer to God asking Him to watch over that person or persons in need will do them just as well.

Be like Jesus and help a friend along. God will bless you for being a blessing.

17

Me and My Friend

Some of these words are from a song I heard, and some are my feelings about it.

This story could be about a couple named Mary and Bob. The words go like this:
Should you go first and I remain
To walk this road alone,
I live with memories of the days we had,
In spring I watch for the roses to bloom,
When days and twilight are blue and in early fall
When brown leaves begin to fall,
I catch a glimpse of you.

Should you go first and I remain
With battles to be fought without you,
For each thing that you touched along the way will be blessed.
I hear your voice and see your smile so blessed
Will I go in the memories of your helping hand?
And joy is beyond hope.

Should you go first and I remain
To finish up this storm alone,

Nothing less than our love shall ever creep in
To make this life seem so fair,
For we have so much love and happiness.
We have had our cup of joy.

Memories are gifts of God
That death cannot destroy.
I want to know each step that you take,
For one day soon I will follow you.

Should you go first and I remain,
One thing I will have you to do.
Walk slowly down that long path,
For soon I will follow you
To that fair land where we will know
No parting, should you go first and I remain.
Look for me for soon
You will hear me calling your name.

If I get there before you do,
Will you walk down that lonely road,
And will you look for my footprints?
Then you will know which way I went,
For I will be looking for you.
For when our work is over here on earth,
We all must travel down that same lonely road.
I will be waiting at that gate for you
And we can go in together.

You will know and see me,
For we have shared so many years together,
And they were such precious years,
I could have never asked for better company.
Our life on earth was as precious as silver and gold,
And we shared them together with much love,
Really, more than our share.

I remember through all the years,
Through hot and cold weather,
You were always there.
I could not have made it without you.
Many times we stumbled along the way,
But we would always pick each other up.
We have shared so many precious years together.
It seemed like we always knew what the other was thinking.
This is the way God meant for it to be.

Some day, when we meet over there,
We will know each other,
For, we will be dressed in a robe of white.
We will have a smile for each other,
And there will be a big field of flowers.
There will be all kinds and all colors.
I have seen them in my dreams.

There will be fields, valleys,
And mountains covered with flowers.
I am looking and waiting for that day to appear.

We will see our loved ones there, too.

If you go first, look for me, for soon I will follow you.

If I go first, I will be looking for you.

There are still a lot of Mary's and Bob's left in this world today. I have seen a lot of couples like this. When one goes, the other soon follows, just like the story says. Their love is so strong that they cannot be without one another. I've seen them when I ride to Griffin and Hampton, Georgia. I wish my life could have been that way.

I think that it is great that two people can love and trust each other like they did. I can still see the old couple just sitting there, happy and loving each other. I see them on the porch. Sometimes they are just swinging together. He will have his arms around her.

I see this every time I go to Hampton, Georgia. Late in the evening the couple sits on the porch and they watch the scenery.

You should try it sometime.

It could be you doing that.

18

Choose the Right Road in Life

My young friend, I would like to share some good, earnest advice with you. I don't mean to meddle in your business, but I am trying to save you from the price you will have to pay if you take the wrong road.

If you could see the truth about things, and see the scars as I have, you would think twice about which road you would choose to travel. I did not get these knots and bruises by lying in bed all day, either. I have been down that wrong road.

You meet bullies who think they are the meanest people around. These types of people usually end up in the graveyard. I have met many of them. Maybe you think that because you are younger, meaner and stronger, that you are a bully too. Just remember there is always a bigger, meaner and stronger person than you.

So young man, be wise and don't get caught up in this world of sin. All that is waiting for you is trouble out there. Be wise and choose the right road to travel.

There are two ways to travel in this life—up or down. Listen to your mom and dad for good advice. Maybe they went down that road, too. If you do not choose the right road to travel, then you may end up like me.

I am 73 years old, and believe me, if I could relive my past, I would. I would have chosen a different path to take.

I am writing this book because a year ago, the Spirit spoke to me and said, "By speaking and telling only people in the church about your testimony, it will not reach the world and be heard by those that may need to hear it. By writing this on paper and putting it in a book, you are enhancing the chances of getting the word out there and you can be of help to some young person."

God does not want us to wind up taking the wrong path, and He does not want us to be content with a sinful lifestyle. He wants us to eventually come to Him and give Him our lives. If your mind is set on running wild in the big city and not listening to the voice of God, then you are bound for heartache. You will just have to learn the hard way.

I wish there were something I could say to you to help you make the right choices in life. My preacher used to say that there are those who hear, but do not receive. Preachers can preach their hearts to people, but if they do not receive the word he preaches, they should have just stayed at home.

Sometimes, when the preacher is preaching a strong message, the people will say, "Boy, he really poured out his heart to us this morning, didn't he?" Then they turn around and ask what the message was about.

Do you know what was happening to those people? They let a little bird fly around their ears and grab the word before they even got it. They were listening to the word but did not receive it. The spirit that was brought forth through the word was missed because they were not receiving the meaning behind the message. They were there physically, but mentally they were removed. That is the way it is in life: some will prosper and some will not.

So, my young friend, make sure that when you sow your seed, you are sowing one that is of value. Sow only good seeds and you will receive blessings. Do not waste all of your precious years. God has given them to you, so use them wisely. Don't do like me and wander around in this world for so many years, just lost. Listen to the one who has wisdom, take his advice and use it to your advantage.

Sow all your seeds in good soil and watch them grow prosperous things. Put all of your trust in God, and not in people here on earth. Listen to the voice of God and receive all the many blessings He has waiting for you.

Do this, so when you get old like me, you can say, "Lord, I have had a good long life. If it were not for that man who wrote that book, I might not be where I am today. Thank you, Lord, for inspiring that man because he has taught me a great lesson in life, and now I am saved. One day, I hope to meet that man who wrote this book and I would like to just shake his hand. I'd like to say, 'thank you, mister, for that message that you wrote in your book. You just might have saved my soul from hell.' I say thanks again, and God bless you."

I hope this story has been a blessing to you. I hope it will make you think twice about the choices you make in life. I hope you always put God first and trust only in His name. May the Lord bless you all, both young and old a like. Go with God and have a good life.

19

Watch Where You Are Walking

This story is about watching where you walk.

It started on July 10, 2006 at 10:15 a.m. I was going down the street in my truck and was making a right turn. I slowed down to make the turn, because there are a lot of people walking, running, or jogging on the road.

After I made my turn, I took off as I normally would. Then, I heard a noise. It turned out that I had hit a man who was walking. I did not see this man who was walking on the road.

My right mirror jammed against my door and this broke the glass in my mirror. I said to myself, "My God, I couldn't have hit that telephone pole."

As I looked back, I saw a man lying in the ditch. I went back and got out of my truck to check on him. He was a big man, about 6 feet 6 inches tall.

I said, "Sir, are you hurt?"

He told me that he wasn't sure. He said that his right side was hurting. That is where my mirror had hit him. His leg had hit my fender.

Across the street, a friend of mine was selling lawn mowers, and he said he saw it all. He said the man was walking on the pavement. But everyone said they didn't think it was my fault.

I have always dreaded that something like that would happen one day, and it did. It was not all my fault, but I did get the ticket. I'm just glad the man was not hurt. I prayed for him, and then my friend, Mack, came from across the street. A man on a bike came on the scene, and he asked the man if he wanted us to pray for him.

The man said, "No, he did not want us to pray for him."

We looked at him.

Then, he said, "Let me catch my breath and then I think I will be okay."

He tried to move, but his right side was hurting too bad.

The police and the EMT had arrived by that time. There was a helicopter flying above, too.

I was given a ticket for failing to yield the right-of-way. I don't mind telling you, I was a little shook up. I was really worried about the man. I wanted him to be okay, not for my sake, but for his. I prayed for him anyway, but silently, to myself.

The man said, "By the way, I'm blind."

I said to myself, "There goes my insurance—it will go sky high!" I had been with my insurance company for twenty-four years, and I have had very few tickets.

Later, I called Jim (the blind man I hit) and he told me that he was walking on the white line because that was all he could see. He told me that when I hit him, all he could see was a big white cloud coming down over him.

I asked him why he was out on that highway walking, with his being blind. He told me that he did it all the time. I asked him if he had any dogs that could walk with him. He said he didn't use them because he was afraid the dogs might get hit. I told him that he should never be out on that road alone without a dog.

Jim told me that they were still running tests on him to make sure he was okay. He said he was only bruised a little. He said he would be back out there walking again in a few weeks, or maybe even in a few days.

I asked him if he was serious about what he had just said, and he said he was. He said that this accident was not going to stop him from walking on that road.

I did tell Jim that the accident could have been a warning to start walking in the park, that he really had no business walking on a busy highway. I told him that if it were me, I would let the accident be a warning. I told him that the road was too busy, and the next time he might not be so lucky.

He told me he had already turned it over to his lawyer.

If a blind man is going to walk out on a road like that, he should have a large sign stating that he is blind, and he should have dogs walking with him to help him see.

I worry, because I do not want to see Jim get killed on that road.

I hope people will be careful and not take risks. The law can only do so much to protect you.

20

Don't Wait Too Long

One time I was following a truck, and it was overloaded. As the driver started going across a bridge, the bridge began to give way. The next thing I knew, the trailer started falling into the water below. It did not fall all the way down, though—it hung on the edge.

The man got out of the truck. We sat there on the bank waiting for a wrecker to come and pull away the wreckage. I talked to him about Jesus. I asked him if he thought it was time for him to accept Jesus Christ as his Lord and Savior.

I knew a little bit about this man already, enough to know that he was not saved. He told me that he was not ready to receive Christ.

Not too long after that, he was in a bad car accident and was killed. He went to meet His maker. I was told later that his wife had a dream, and she had the same dream three nights in a row. She saw her husband and he was in hell. In the dream, he told her he had the chance to receive Jesus as his Savior, but had passed on the opportunity to do so. He said that he was now burning in hell, and he was being tormented day after day. He also told her that he would be there for eternity.

He begged her to accept Christ and not make the same mistake that he did, because he did not want her to have to burn in hell as he was. He asked her to tell his loved ones about the dream, and of everything he told her, so they could be saved from the pain he was experiencing.

He said, "If I could just relive my life, I would have called on Jesus, and would not be here burning in hell."

Believe me, my friend, hell is real and is not something to take lightly. When you get sick here on earth and you are in so much pain, it can't compare to what hell would be like.

When you are cast into hell or the lake of fire, it will be far too late to turn around and call on Jesus. Come now, my friend, while there is still time. Don't procrastinate when it comes to taking the hand of God when He offers it to you. Don't say," tomorrow", because you are not guaranteed a tomorrow, or another second for that matter.

If you are not saved, you can be sure that changing your life and giving it to Christ will be the best thing you can ever do for yourself. All you have to do is believe in your heart and confess with your mouth that Jesus Christ is Lord and Savior, and He died on a cross to save our souls. He died so that we may live prosperous and abundant lives here on earth.

If it means giving up all the earthly pleasures you now have, then I would say, "go for it!"

The joy of the Lord cannot be taken away, regardless of what you do or do not have here on earth. Just remember that not everybody will get a second chance to make their lives right with God.

Two times in my life I thought that I was going from this earth. So let me tell you, it is not a good feeling to have. I believe I will go to Heaven, because I do try to the best of my ability to be on the best terms I possibly can with our Father God.

Maybe you don't want to have to worry about whether or not you are going to make it. The only way to do that is to live by the laws of Christ. I try my best to stay in line with God. I live for Jesus now. When I was younger, I was out in the world running with nothing but a sinful nature. But I am glad that God has given me another chance, a chance to be redeemed and live for Him. When Jesus came back into my life, I made a full turn around, and that is what it will take to stay out of hell.

So, if you do not know Jesus, please do not wait any longer to accept Him. Remember that tomorrow may never come, so don't wait for tomorrow to be the day you accept Him.

Choose Christ today!

God bless you and keep you safe.

Jesus loves you.

21

A Story about a Funeral

I was walking down the streets in Shreveport Louisiana one Sunday morning. I had slept in the park that night and I was cold and hungry. As I walked that way, I heard the sound of an organ playing an old, sad song. As I reached the church, I looked in the window, and my heart went out to them.

As I was listening, I found myself inside that church. I saw then that there was a funeral being held. Up front there was a man and a woman sitting with their heads bowed low. There was a small casket with a small child inside, a little boy.

I could picture that little fellow running around and living a good life. He had curly hair and a smiling face, and he was running and playing.

I have seen a lot of funerals in my life. In the front of the church was a gray haired preacher. Around him, and around the casket, were some roses. As he stood behind the pulpit, he had a slight smile on his face and a sad look in his eyes. He told everyone not to weep for the little boy that was lying there in the casket, for he does not live here anymore, but he is gone to a better place.

The preacher said, "Now, that little boy loved you all and would have loved to stay here for a long time with all of you, but the good Lord loved him too, and came to take him to that big house up above.

"The Lord knows that you loved him and took good care of him. The Lord thought that all of you needed a little sunshine, and He let you borrow this child for a while, until your hearts got so full of love that they could burst.

"The Lord sees those tears that you are shedding. Now, just think of all the joy, love and good times you had together while little Bobby was down here with you. The Lord sees so much further than we can down the road. Just maybe the good Lord saved little Bobby from hell. Think about that. Remember, God never does anything without a reason."

He continued, "Try to always look on the bright side of life. I do know that it hurts now, but later you will see that when God took Bobby, it was the right choice.

"So, mom, dad and friends, if you are living for Jesus, just remember that one day you will see little Bobby again. One day soon, Jesus is coming back and that little one will be with Him. For Jesus has promised that He will come back for us."

I can see Him coming everyday when I look up in the sky. Look up, my friend, look to the sky and see the clouds. Don't be afraid to look for Jesus up in the clouds. That is where His heaven is.

One day, I will see His whole body coming down from the heavens, and you will go there too, if you live for Jesus. Living for Jesus is so much better than living for the devil.

Remember, the only hope we have to see our loved ones again is to live for Jesus. I know it seems that God is so far away, but He isn't if he lives in your heart. If you look for God, you will surely find Him. God is everywhere.

I have known families that have lost loved ones, and it seems they cannot let go of their memory. That is why you need God in your life. Just put your trust in Him—there is no other way.

I do know that many people do not believe in God, so they say. But let them get in trouble, and they will call on Him first.

I knew a man in Greenville, Georgia who had a foul tongue. One day, he had chest pain and fell to the floor. He did not believe in God. But the first thing he said was, "God, have mercy on me."

The doctor told him it was indigestion. The first thing he did was start cursing again. He didn't realize that God heard him. I have always wondered why people think they can slip things by God. He knows all, and sees and hears all.

I took a truck to Maaco to be painted, and I asked the man there if he liked Gospel music. He said no, he did not believe in God and that he was an atheist.

I said, "You are a what?"

And he said it again. "I'm an atheist."

I told him that he just <u>thought</u> he didn't believe in God. I asked him if I could tell him a story about a man like him.

He agreed, so I told him the story about the man in Greenville, Georgia with the chest pains, and how the first thing he did was call on God.

You see, every knee shall bow and every tongue shall confess that Jesus Christ is Lord. There is no other God before Him. He is the beginning and the end.

I told him, "Now, don't tell me that you don't believe in God. I am going to leave a tape on the desk and every time you walk around that desk, it will be staring at you."

I told him that he needed God. He said, "Yeah, I need Him bad, don't I?"

I told him that not everyone gets a second chance. Sometimes God just calls you right out. Don't be fooled by people who tell you there is no God.

When you lose someone close to you, just know that God knows best.

Now, don't weep for that little fellow. For it won't be long until Jesus comes, and when He comes, that little child will be with Him. Rejoice and be glad; soon Jesus will make everything all right.

22

Adam's Farm

This story is about business people and friends of mine.

There is a lady named Virginia who owns Adam's Farm. I have been buying the biggest tomatoes from her. She also sells peaches and all kinds of vegetables, along with homemade jellies and honey.

You can slice one of the tomatoes and use only one slice to make a good sandwich. I love fresh vegetables, so have eaten my share of them, as well as the peaches.

The market is in a good location, right off of Highway 54 in Fayetteville, Georgia.

Virginia also sings in a quartet. It is called the Sweet Inspirations. They go around to different churches and sing.

Once, I gave Virginia one of my tapes (I sing a little). She listened and asked me to come and sing along with them at a concert they were having in Fayetteville. She told me of Johnny Cochran holding a concert at his home on May 13. She called and asked Johnny if I could sing with them, and I had a chance to go down and meet him.

After that, Johnny told me he would let me sing, and he tried to put me in last since he was already filled up. He said if that worked out, I could sing a couple of songs.

I did get the chance to go, and I met several Nashville stars and singers from around Georgia. I met a lot of people there.

Johnny is a great man. I had never met him before, and I don't know why, because we have been living so close to each other for such a long time. But, ever since we have met, we have been great friends.

The songs I sang were "You Win Again" and "The Ring of Fire." Boy, that was a great experience for me because I had never sung in a concert before! There were a lot of pretty girls singing there, too. They all seemed to have enjoyed my performance. It makes you feel really good when people clap their hands and cheer you on.

We had a special star from Nashville and a long-time friend of Johnny's who was there. I had my picture taken with her. She was just as sweet as she could be, and pretty too. I hope to see every one of them next year. I will learn some new songs and be ready for them.

When I went to see my son, he asked me if I needed a manager and could he have my autograph.

"Of course," I said.

If you are ever down in Fayetteville, don't forget to stop at Adam's Farm and load up on the vegetables, jellies and peaches.

23

The Chicken, Girls and "Taters"

Now, there are three girls working at this place—Debbie, Brenda and Pat. This is not the same Brenda mentioned earlier in my love story.

These are very sweet ladies. They sell fried chicken, chicken wings, corn on the cob and corn dogs, among other things. You name it—they've got it!

They stay very busy.

To me, we are all just like one big family. Every time I make a tape, I take them one. They listen to it and they tell me what they think.

I am always stopping by there to "pick" at them, telling them about my past with some of my old girlfriends, and some women I have met.

When I walk in, I cut loose with a song. They say, "Here comes that wild man."

I love those girls. The reason I call the women "girls" is because I don't want them to get old, like me. Besides, you are only as old as you feel.

Well, Debbie, Pat and Brenda, keep up the good work. Keep cooking that chicken and other good food. Always remember to rattle those pots and pans.

See you'll later.
Have a nice day.

24

Hester's Petro

Now, this is another place across the from Adam's Farm. It is called Hester's Petro. Mr. Hester sells the best sausage and biscuits, better than anyone around there. Once you have had a biscuit at Hester's place, you can't stop eating them.

I go by Hester's almost every morning to get some of those tasty biscuits and sausage. Sometimes, I switch it up and get bacon and biscuits. You name it—Hester's got it!

Hester and his wife, Faye, have three children—two girls and one boy. I have only seen his boy one time.

The family is a group of hard workers, and for as long as I have known them, they have been the kindest people I know. I think the world of them, because these days, it is hard to find such good friends. Being friends with them has taught me to hold on to good people when you find them.

My son started going to Hester's long before I did. He was the one who told me about them. They are all very good to my son. They always ask about him.

I would like to say to Hester and his family—keep up the good work. You have a great place. Mary, Shirley and Faye, keep cooking those good biscuits and other things.

I want you to know that you are a great bunch of people

25

The Eagle and the Barnyard Chicken

An eagle rises above everything, and flies above adversity and problems. It can see the whole picture.

So many times, we become like the barnyard chicken in our problems. We can't get out of the pen, and we pray and pray, but we can't seem to fly above the fence. It seems that we are held in that place that seems to have no way out.

When an eagle begins to lose its feathers on its wings, it can't fly like before.

We are like that eagle who can't fly like before—we look up from the chicken coop and see the skies as far as we can see. We remember that we could fly above everything, high into the heavens, knowing that our creator made us to be lifted up above all circumstances.

Jesus Christ overcame, and so can we. We belong to Him. That longing comes back into the eagle (us) and we begin to rise, and our strength is renewed. We begin to feel the freedom and how we could once see quite a distance.

There are times when we begin to take our eyes off the One who gave us the freedom (Son), and we lower our vision and begin to lose the place we had come to in the Lord. We begin to get caught up in the religious order, and we like all the hype and excitement of that realm.

We drop down in the chicken coop (conformity) with the crowds.

An eagle flies alone or with its mate. Not many want to come into that place. But the eagle saints have discernment, and they can see into all that is not like Him (Jesus Christ), the only source from our Father God. Jesus said, "... we sit in heavenly places with Him." (Ephesians 2:6)

Although it is finished and the work is done, we have to ascend into that place. We have to come to an experience of this and manifest it in our lives. As He begins to open our eyes of understanding, He reveals the truth of who He is. (Ephesians 1:18)

We wait for more of Him, and then we become loosed from what holds us in a place. We begin to mount up and fly.

The mountains (problems) become flat. The crooked places become straight. Light shines in the darkness, and the darkness becomes light.

We see clearly and we begin to breathe in the purity of God.

We no longer listen to the chicken telling us that we can't get out of the pen (problem), that we belong with them.

You say, "Chicken, I have seen Him whom my soul loveth, high and lifted up, and He says I can fly, and I can come and sit with Him and eat of Him and drink of Him. He lives in me and moves in me and I have my being in Him."

Many will try to stop you and tell you it is not possible, but he said streams of life will begin to flow out of you. Flesh gives birth to flesh and spirit gives birth to spirit.

You say, "This is all I've known."

He says, "You are a new creation, and I have much more for you. I'll remove the veil from your eyes."

You say, "Lord, I have heart problems and sickness."

He says, "I took stripes for your healing."

You say, "But I am grieving; my husband has died and I am alone."

He says, "You're not alone. I am with you and I came to comfort those that grieve."

You say, "I don't have money for food and for my children."

He says, "I own the cattle on a thousand hills and all is Mine. I have food you know not of."

You say, "My son is an alcoholic."

He says, "I came to set the captives free."

The creator of this heaven and earth and all that is in it (man included) rides on the clouds and says, "Drop rain here, and let My words begin to soak in the heart of man." When He thunders forth His orders out of the heavens, they obey. (Ephesians 4:22)

Put off the old self, which is being corrupted by the deceitful desires (the barnyard chicken which cannot look any higher than the chicken pen [problem]), and be made new in the attitude of your mind. The new self, created to be like God in true righteousness and holiness. Like the eagle, you can soar into new places in Him, above the deceitful desires. (Psalms 103:5)

He satisfies my desires with good things, so that my youth is renewed like the eagle's. If we stay on the lower plane, we will be so buffeted about by the winds of adversity, fear, the threat of carnal thinking, and the weakness of our own body, that soon our eagle feathers will be trampled upon. They will be broken off, making it impossible for us to fly.

The Bible is full of stories of men and women, like myself who were mounted up with wings like eagles, transforming their lives from a lowly state into a higher and more glorious state. It was the more glorious state that Jesus was referring to when He said, "I am come that they might have life and have it more abundantly." And that is the state of being that I live in today.

The End

Names of Those Who Have Given Permission For Their Names in the Book

Steve Whitlock, Sheriff of Meriwether County

Brandon Bulloch, Deputy Sheriff of Meriwether County

Jason Ritter, Deputy Sheriff of Meriwether County

Bruce O'Neal, Director of Public Works of Meriwether County

Virginia Adams

Anita Beckom

Bobby Beckom

Carla Beckom

Catherine Beckom

Jack Beckom

James Beckom, Jr.

Jerry Beckom

Johnny Cochran

Milton Beckom

Perry Beckom

Tiffany Beckom

Tommy Beckom

Johnny Cochran

Brenda Couch

Patricia Cooper

Brandy Hester

Faye Hester

W. E. Hester

Shirley Johnson

Larry Jones

Melvin Jones

Robert Jones

Debbie Kohl

Mary Nolan

Billy Peterman

Janelle Peterman

Ida Smallwood

Lee South

Mary Ann South

978-0-595-44512-7
0-595-44512-8

Printed in the United States
88093LV00003B/127-162/A